PRAISE FOR

"Everything about Jim's early life should have prepared him to fail in his professional and personal life. Instead, he succeeded on both dimensions on an unparalleled scale. And despite the title of his book, his success had nothing to do with luck. His life story is inspiring and the insights that Jim shares with readers should be required reading for any entrepreneur."

—Chuck Esserman,
CEO and founder of TSG Consumer Partners

"The most impressive thing about Jim Markham isn't how many brands he's built or how much money he's made. It's how many lives he's touched (including mine) and how much loyalty and love he has garnered in a tumultuous and sometimes difficult life. The people he hires come back to work for him again and again. His story is not just a riveting tale of success, fame, and fortune but equally the things that matter even more in life: work, love, and family."

—Yasser Toor,
Former Managing Director TSG Consumer Partners

"Jim Markham's career has been fascinating to watch, and I had a front row seat for an important part of it. As Jim took over Sebring, my association with him had a major impact on my life, career, and success. *Big Lucky* is a perfect example of how you can create your own luck with determination and grit."

—Patricia Fripp, CSP, CPAE,
Past President National Speakers Association

"An inspiring story of triumph over trauma, *Big Lucky* will leave readers believing anything is possible and that it's never too late for a new beginning."

—Julie Cantrell,
New York Times and *USA TODAY*
bestselling author of *Perennials*

"Rarely have I come across a more unimaginable life story than Jim Markham's. He takes us from the depths of his fear as a ninth-grade dropout with a pregnant 15-year-old wife to his triumph as an award-winning hair stylist to the stars like Steve McQueen and Paul Newman to his journey as a visionary serial entrepreneur in the hair care industry. Along the way he shares the hard-won lessons he's learned as he encountered almost every tough break you can imagine: from losing everything in a partnership gone bad to being homeless. His raw and inspirational story and his determination to manifest the life that he longed for will inspire all those dreamers out there to keep believing—no matter how many times you get knocked down."

—Kathy L. Murphy,
founder of the Pulpwood Queens Book Club, who named *Big Lucky*
one of her 2020 top picks for her 800+ chapter book club

BIG LUCKY

SERIAL ENTREPRENEUR
JIM MARKHAM'S SECRET FORMULA
FOR SUCCESS

JIM MARKHAM

WITH ECHO MONTGOMERY GARRETT

Published in the United States by Jim Markham Enterprises, Inc.
Copyright © Jim Markham Enterprises, Inc., 2020
First Edition All rights reserved. Printed in the United States.
This title is also available in an audio book and e-book via the Publisher Jim Markham
Enterprises, Inc. (BigLucky@jimmarkham.com)
Cover & interior design: Prominence Publishing
Cover photo: Fabrizio Maltese
Mechanical editor: Wade Baker
Authors' photos: Fabrizio Maltese and Jason Randazzo

A Note to the Reader: Every effort has been made to ensure that the information contained in
this book is complete and accurate. The content is based on the personal experiences of the
author and interviews with many of his family members, friends, and business associates. It
is published for general reference and education with the intent of inspiring hope, increasing
resilience and offering encouragement. The book is sold with the understanding that neither
the authors nor publisher is engaged in rendering any professional services including legal,
psychological, career or medical advice to the individual reader. The authors and publisher
specifically disclaim any liability, loss, damage, injury or risk, directly or indirectly, for advice,
suggestions and information presented within. Neither the authors nor the publisher assumes
responsibility for errors, inaccuracies, omissions, or inconsistencies. Some of the names and
identifying details of people mentioned in this book have been changed.

LCCN: 2021903482
Markham, Jim, 1943-present
Garrett, Echo Montgomery, 1960-present
BIG LUCKY: SERIAL ENTREPRENEUR JIM MARKHAM'S SECRET FORMULA FOR
SUCCESS/Jim Markham, Echo Montgomery Garrett
ISBN: 978-1-7344951-2-6
1. Memoir 2. Entrepreneurship 3. Self Help 4. Success 5. Life Lessons 6. Celebrities 7. Hair
Care Industry 8. Overcoming poverty 9. Partnerships 10. Love Story 11. Family business
12. Parental alienation 13. Leadership 14. Addiction 15. Positive Thinking

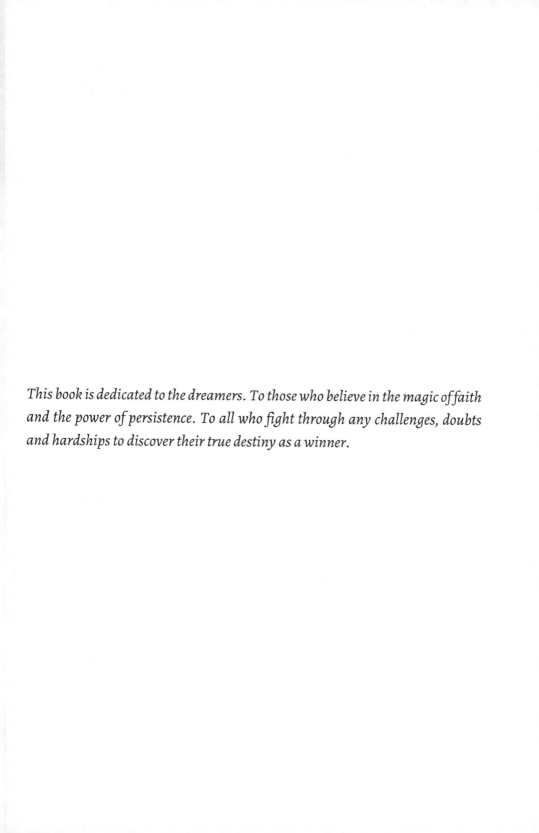

This book is dedicated to the dreamers. To those who believe in the magic of faith and the power of persistence. To all who fight through any challenges, doubts and hardships to discover their true destiny as a winner.

TABLE OF CONTENTS

MY ROOTS

My good friend and life mentor, the late Paul Newman, used to say there are three kinds of luck: big luck, little luck, and no luck. With his famous blue eyes twinkling, he once handed me a bowl of his latest kitchen creation—popcorn and jicama—and said, "Markham, you are Big Lucky."

Maybe he was right.

I now know, I was made to win, even though the odds had been stacked against me from the very beginning.

I experienced immeasurable difficulties in my childhood. At 15, I was married and a father. To support my family, I started cutting hair.

My mentor, Jay Sebring, famed stylist to the stars, was murdered by the Manson Family, leaving me some big shoes to fill.

I was homeless at different points in my life and I had to start over more than once.

In this book, I'm telling the story like it is—the good, the bad, and the ugly, for one reason: **I want you to understand that you are made to win, too**.

You see, at every low point of my life, I refused to quit. That determination brought me to high points I could have never imagined. Over the course of my career, I've been at the helm of five successful hair care companies. To date, the combined retail sales of these companies has topped $1.2 billion, and that number continues to climb.

As a serial entrepreneur, I pioneered several breakthrough products in the hair care industry—products that earned me many awards including Ernst & Young's *Entrepreneur of the Year* and Intercoiffure's *Lifetime Achievement Icon Award.*

I say all this not to blow my own horn, but to make the point that if you're willing to put in the time and effort to make your dreams a reality, then you can do anything with your life—absolutely anything.

INTRODUCTION

JIM MARKHAM'S 22 KEY INGREDIENTS FOR LONG-LASTING SUCCESS

W hen you get up in the morning and look in the mirror, what's your first thought? Do you focus on what you don't like about yourself or do you see a person you care about and are rooting for—a person made to win?

I've spent my entire career helping others feel better about their appearance. As the highest-paid celebrity hair stylist, my clients trusted me with one of their most important assets—their looks. For decades, I cut and styled some of the world's most beautiful people.

What did I learn from working with stars at the top of their game? They believed they were made to win. They all shared that drive, that fire, to be the very best.

I was surprised to discover many of the world's most admired celebrities and many of my peers had survived difficult childhoods, much like me.

Iconic movie star and my client Steve McQueen, for example, was abandoned by his parents and sent to reform school in his early teens before making his way into acting. My friend Vidal Sassoon spent seven years in an orphanage before landing an apprenticeship with a London stylist. The rest is history.

I quickly realized the one thing that united us all was our determination to win regardless of our backgrounds. These stories helped me feel less alone and fueled my belief in myself—convincing me that no matter how difficult my background had been, I could create the future of my dreams.

I write this book today with the hopes that by sharing my story, I can help you achieve even greater success in your life.

INGREDIENT #1

PAIN CAN FUEL
YOU FORWARD

I could tell my mother Ruby was getting ready to go out for the night. She'd secured her strawberry blonde hair with a generous dose of hairspray, dabbed on the perfume that made my nose itch, and put on her cherry-red dress with matching splash of lipstick.

"I made your favorite, Jimbo," she said, cheerfully placing a plate of my favorite comfort food in front of me: chicken fried steak and country mashed potatoes.

With gratitude, I ate every last bite. But I was anything but comforted. My stomach continued to churn, as I eyed the slim stack of dollar bills on the kitchen table.

I knew what that money meant.

Mom worked as a waitress and a short-order cook whenever she could get the hours. With Christmas coming, her tips had been extra good. She kissed me goodnight on my forehead and said, "Be a good boy."

She swung the front door open wide, allowing a blast of cold air to send a shiver down my spine. "Good night," she said with a hopeful smile. "Don't let the bed bugs bite." Then the door slammed behind her, and off she went into the dark New Mexico night.

Unlike other kids, I'd learned early on to dread the holidays. No glimmering tree. No wrapped presents. No Christmas miracles. What made it worse was that my birthday was a few days before Christmas, which meant that went overlooked, too. All the season brought me was more time alone while Mom danced and drank herself into the arms of whatever stranger happened to be around for last call.

I hated the silence and the dark that settled over our tiny house that night. I must have been around age five, because I hadn't started school yet. Outside, oil rigs dotted the countryside of Hobbs, and there was no getting away from the heavy smell of sulfur. I hated that smell, too.

Even though I could see my breath inside the house, I turned on the swamp cooler and twirled the dial of my transistor radio until some sad-sack country song crackled through the static. But no matter how loud I turned the dial, it did nothing to change the fact that once again I was cold. I was alone. And I was afraid.

Starting school the next year was a relief, but not because I enjoyed learning. I'd never even seen a book, and I certainly didn't know my alphabet or my numbers. But it gave me somewhere to go besides the empty house. With the Army Air Base near Hobbs and the transient oil workers shuffling through town, there was always some new kid showing up at Edison Elementary. Each time I'd get my hopes up. *Maybe this one will like me.*

I was one of the smallest kids in the class, despite being almost seven by the time I started first grade—a choice my mother had made due to my late-in-the-year birthday. My mom had always been petite and baby-faced, and I took after her—meaning I attracted the attention of bullies.

There were always bullies to be found, but one day, in the second grade, one of the meanest of them all decided to befriend me. Older than me by a couple years, and taller by a good foot or two, he insisted on accompanying me for the seven-block walk home. My new friend towered above me as we made our way toward Mom's most recent rental house—a shack, really—one of the four identical 500-square-foot cabins built for oil yard workers who preferred to stay on the outskirts of town.

We talked for the first few blocks, scuffing our tattered shoes in the sand along the way. Then, near the halfway point, he suddenly snatched my pencil, broke it in half and shredded the paper my mom was supposed to sign. Grabbing me by the shoulders, he whirled me around to face him. With a satisfied smirk, he punched me hard in the face. Three times.

My fair cheeks, already burned red by the desert sun, heated with a mix of anger and shame. I tucked tail and ran to what I calculated to be a safe distance. Then I stopped, turned back around and began hurling rocks at him with all my might. I wanted to hurt him like he hurt me, but he simply laughed and walked away.

That wasn't the last time I would know such pain.

With my mother off on one of her benders, I had no way of knowing when she'd come home again. I was anxious about spending the 20 cents she'd left behind, so I carefully weighed my options. I was hungry, but I was too angry to eat. What I really needed was an escape, so I spent those dimes on a ticket to the movies. I started with the matinee and stayed until the theater shut down for the night. While I dreaded the long walk home in the darkness, anything was better than the silent hours alone.

To be honest, I don't know what was worse, the long hours spent alone or the chaos that seemed to happen when Mom was around. One wintry night, she suddenly woke me up to announce an impromptu trip to visit my grandparents. By then, I'd learned we only visited my grandparents when we had to hurry and leave because the rent was coming due. This time, while en route to her home state of Oklahoma, she wheeled off the highway into the parking lot of a busy bar somewhere near Big Springs, Texas. "I'll be right back," she called, slamming the car door behind her.

I kept my eyes on the bar room, watching the people coming and going, expecting my mother to emerge soon. She'd promised.

After what seemed like an eternity, I finally spotted her—unsteady, cheeks flushed. "We're going for a little ride," she said, slurring her words and swerving back onto the highway behind a dark sedan.

A few blocks away, she turned into a neighborhood with some of the nicest houses I'd ever seen. "Wait here, Jimbo," she said, scraping the tires as she parked too close against the curb.

After a while, I sat up on my knees, watching for her. The passenger window fogged up again and again. Each time I took the edge of my shirt and rubbed a circle so I could see out. I sketched a design with my fingers. I drew a mom and dad, smiling in front of a house. Then I wiped it away.

By now, the sun had been replaced by the moon and it was dark and I didn't have a jacket or a blanket, so I grew colder and colder, teeth chattering. Gazing at the stars, I concentrated on the points of light, trying to stitch together patterns while I talked to the moon.

My eyes grew heavy from exhaustion, my ears and toes ached from the cold, and my eyes nearly froze shut with tears as I wished for the warmth of my bed. I sang and made up stories, trying to pass the time. But as the hours dragged by, I finally decided to go look for her.

I crept out of the car and I realized I'd forgotten which house she'd entered. One by one, I started knocking on doors in the dark. Nobody answered.

Well after the sun was up, shaking uncontrollably with a terrible mix of cold, fear and anger, I finally saw my mother come out of one of the houses. Squinting in the sunlight and smoothing her dress, she walked toward me. Then she got in the car without a word.

My stomach rumbled with hunger. "I was cold, Mama. I didn't know where you were."

"Oh, you were fine," she said, casually lighting a cigarette and cranking the car. "Just fine."

By the time I turned 12, I'd sometimes get fed up. I'd take the two- or three-mile walk—depending on what place she'd found to rent at the time—to search the bars lining the roughneck oil town. Usually, I'd slow to admire the Chevys at the car dealership as I trudged past. I always liked the shiny new cars. The '55s in red and white trim were my favorite.

The kind, generous, and loving mother I had when Mom was sober was nowhere to be found on these searches. Instead, I'd find her wild-eyed alter ego, hanging all over whatever man had caught her attention for the night.

"C'mon, Mom, let's go," I'd say, pulling her away from her latest mistake. Most evenings she'd fight me and then invariably the man, likely expecting a payout for the few dollars he'd spent at the bar, would give me an angry shove. My biggest fear was she'd be beat up or killed, or me—or both of us.

I spent those early years feeling lonely, and most of all, afraid. The men my mother brought home always made it clear I was a bother. Some let me know it by beating me.

More times than I'd like to count, I woke up to the sharp sting of some stranger's belt slapping me across the back. The man of the evening would shout that he needed privacy, kicking me out of the house while Mom looked on swaying to some tune only she could hear. With glassy eyes and tousled hair, no amount of perfume could shroud the heavy scent of her cigarettes or the stale reek of alcohol.

If I didn't vacate fast enough, she would join in, yelling while slapping at me, "Get out, boy. Get out now." She practically spit the words.

My father—named Albert Carter Markham, but everybody called him A.C.—was never there to protect me. During my earliest years before my parents' divorce, they managed a country store in Edinburg, Texas. I have only a few memories of my dad living with us, but I do remember vividly the day he came home to discover another man in bed with my mom. The man looked like a giant as my dad dragged him past me out onto the front lawn. My mom ran flailing and shrieking close behind, her pink robe flapping around her.

The big guy kept scrambling on top of my dad, beating him badly as the two men tussled across the sunbaked caliche dirt. He was hurting my daddy, and I wanted him to stop. I picked up a big, heavy stone, lifted it as high as my little arms could manage, and waited for my chance to drop it on the bad man's head. Just as I let go, the man rolled out of striking distance. The rock dropped with a hard thud in the dirt, barely missing my bare feet.

I don't remember Dad being around much after that.

My father was a two-pack-a-day Marlboro man and heavy equipment operator, a serious-minded workaholic, a man of few words.

Dad had grown up in Arkansas, where he got caught running moonshine when he was barely into his teens. For that, he was sent away to reform school until some neighbors petitioned for his release five years later. He'd been on the right side of the law ever since.

Most of my youth, I lived with my mother, but from time to time, my father would come through New Mexico on different construction jobs. He brought with him my older brother, Bobby.

Dad rented a decent house in a respectable neighborhood, and I moved in with them. I was excited to have an older brother to watch over me and show me the ropes.

Bobby and I had been in the same household less than a week when I figured out that his idea of being a big brother and my idea of what that meant didn't match up. I wanted. . . I needed a protective mentor. He, on the other hand, had decided I needed to be toughened up.

On a daily basis, he made me run, do pull-ups, push-ups, chin-ups and stomach crunches. Even worse, he set up wrestling and boxing matches with his middle school buddies. I became their punching bag, and most of the matches ended with me in a mess of bruises and a puddle of tears.

The first few times I got beat down, I looked at my brother, expecting him to step in. He never did.

Then, something happened. Dad bought me a bike. I got my first taste of freedom.

I rode my bike almost every day after school, pumping as fast as I could and loving the feeling of the wind against my face. One afternoon I was racing down this big hill near my home. I looked both ways and didn't see anything coming. I ran the stop sign and a car T-boned me—sending me flying through the air before landing flat on my back hard on a patch of asphalt.

Miraculously, my bike was the only casualty. I had so much adrenaline pumping that I jumped up and started trying to ride away, even though my front wheel was now shaped like an egg.

"Are you okay?" the driver shouted, leaping from the car with great concern.

I had no idea if I was okay. All I knew was the overwhelming fear that my dad was going to be mad because my bike was all bungled up. The man put my bike in his trunk and drove me home. His brows pinched tight with worry as he asked me again and again if I was hurt.

Dad took one look at me and never bothered to ask if I was okay. The man insisted they take me to the hospital, but my dad nixed that idea immediately, saying, "Oh, he'll be all right. He's tougher than he looks."

"Well then, at least let me pay for a new bike," said the man, frowning. He wrote my dad a check for the full amount. "This should cover it."

Dad accepted the check, shook the man's hand, and that was that. My father bought me a new bike, and I was just grateful not to be in trouble.

When I was 12 years old, Mom was involved with yet another new man and Dad got a job to haul a load of watermelons all the way from Hobbs to Anchorage, Alaska. His wife, Lenora, who he'd married and divorced twice already, was going to ride in the cab with him and 17-year-old Bobby had decided to stay in Hobbs with his new wife. "You want to come along, Jimsted?" My father asked, using the nickname he'd given me when I was little. "You're welcome to ride in the back with the watermelons."

That sounded like the most exciting thing ever. All I could think about was going somewhere far, far away from New Mexico. Plus, I'd get to be on an adventure with my dad!

I began counting the days before our trip. Then, less than a week before we were scheduled to leave, my buddy and I came across some horses in a pasture and decided it would be a good idea to ride them. When we led them near the road, the horse I was riding got spooked by a passing car. The horse shied and threw me off, snapping my collarbone like a matchstick.

When it came time for the road trip, I climbed into the back of the truck with Dad's load of watermelons and my broken bone. He built a little pallet for me, but we'd barely made it outside of Hobbs before I cried uncle. The truck's vibration was jarring the pallet and I was on fire with pain.

I fought to hold back tears until I could stand it no more, finally confessing I was in too much agony from the bouncing of the bed of the truck to be able to complete the trip. I was truly disappointed.

Shortly after, dad announced that he'd be moving from Hobbs to take a new job in Farmington. "Your mother just got remarried," he said. "I guess you'll be living with them."

The news hit me like a double punch to the gut. Perhaps it was his way of saying he was sorry for abandoning me yet again, he drove me to Sears & Roebuck and bought me a brand-new scooter. Then he dropped me off at my mom's doorstep, saying simply, "This way you'll have some transportation, Jimsted."

If he'd only known, the only place I wanted to go was with him.

Takeaways

- We'll all meet bullies along our path.
- We have NO control over another person's choices or behaviors.
- Sometimes, the people we love the most are the ones who hurt us the most.
- We can love someone without allowing them to destroy us.

INGREDIENT #2

YOU CAN'T OUTRUN TROUBLE

Mom's new husband's name was Basil. He hated me on sight. After moving in with Mom and Basil, my only consolation was that their house was on the opposite side of town, affording me the opportunity to make friends at a new school —which I did. One of those friends, Ronnie Mahan, often invited me to his house. We rode scooters together every day. For the first time in my life, I was in control. I could go where I wanted to when I wanted to. I was free!

His dad worked in the oil field like most men in town; his mom smelled nice and smiled a lot. She often greeted us with a plate full of chocolate chip cookies fresh from the oven. The Mahan family was as close to perfect as any I'd ever seen, so I hung around as much as possible and was often invited to stay for dinner.

Meanwhile, at my house, the chaos continued. Not long after I moved in with Mom and Basil, they got blind drunk and wound up in a knockdown, drag-out fight. I tried to make them stop, but Basil clocked Mom—breaking her glasses and opening a big gash just under her left eye. Blood flew across the kitchen as my mother screamed.

The next morning, they were lovey-dovey again like nothing had ever happened. But I wasn't so quick to forget. That afternoon, while coming home from school, I spotted Basil down an alleyway. I filled my hands with rocks from the ground and rushed toward him, hurling the stones his way with force just as I'd done to my elementary school bully. Enraged, Basil didn't react the same way. Instead, he stormed my way, ready for a fight. Realizing I'd made a big mistake, I quickly dodged him, disappearing down another alley.

Sick of the bullies—the drunken men, my brother's friends, and now my stepfather—I was ready to fight. Shortly afterwards, I found out our local Boys Club offered boxing lessons. I started to train and I got pretty good.

Not long into summer, Basil issued an ultimatum: Either I go or he goes.

My mother chose him.

With most of her family too distant or dysfunctional, I was sent to live with my older half-sister, Betty Jo, and her mean-as-a-snake husband, Howard, for the remaining summer months.

Twelve years my elder, Betty Jo might as well have been a stranger. She lived way out in the Oklahoma countryside and had rarely ever visited us. She and Howard operated a small farm, and my task was to milk the cows and gather eggs before sunup every morning.

I didn't mind the work and the animals became steady companions, especially the scraggly barn kittens that seemed to always be in need of attention. One particular calico relied on me as her nursemaid, and I took the role seriously. Then one day, a cow stepped on the little kitten I'd been nursing back to health. Try as I might, I couldn't get the cow to lift her hoof. Desperate, I grabbed a Coke bottle and began hitting the cow with all my might. She bolted out of the barn, but it was too late. My kitten was a goner.

Sobbing, I hurled the bottle as high and hard as I could toward the beast who'd killed the little kitten. To my surprise, that bottle came down right in between the cow's eyes, causing her to drop immediately to her knees. Then she keeled over.

I'd done it now! Betty Jo's husband—a brutal man I refused to call my uncle—was going to tan my hide with a riding crop if he found out I'd killed one of his three valuable cows! I weighed my options: Lie. Run away. Lie *and* run away.

That's when something crazy happened. The cow—the cow I thought I'd just killed with a Coke bottle—suddenly woke up and lumbered back to her feet. Now, I'd never been to church, but I was pretty sure what I just witnessed was God's miracle.

Not long after that, just before school started, I was shipped back to Farmington, New Mexico, where my mom had landed after her marriage to Basil had busted up.

There wasn't a whole lot of difference between Hobbs and Farmington. Both had sprung up around the post-World War Two oil boom. Both were populated with wildcatters, roughnecks, Indians, Mexicans, and cowboys. And both were real rough-and-tumble places where a vulnerable woman like my mom found plenty of men willing to buy her as many drinks as she wanted.

By this time, Dad had blown back into Farmington too, and was set up in a camper-trailer just outside of town. He and his wife Lenora were busted up again. He picked a spot three miles outside of town on top of a mountain. With only one bed and a tiny kitchen, there was scarcely room for two of us to be in the camper at the same time, but I still tried to spend as much time with him as he'd tolerate.

At 13 years of age, I also began to notice girls, so I started to focus all my attention in that direction while trying to ignore all the chaos happening with my parents. Once after school, I stayed to work on homework with a pretty, dark-haired girl in my class. I'd had a crush on her for a while, and I was desperate to impress her. With sincere intentions, I worked out a difficult algebra problem and showed her how to get to the answer. The next day, when we turned in our homework, the teacher called me to the front of the class and claimed there was no way I could have come up with the right answer. He accused me of cheating and marked my paper with a big red F.

I could feel my face turning red and that familiar flame of fury tightening my throat. *He thinks I'm stupid.* No matter how hard I tried to succeed, school felt like one of those desert dust storms. Anxiety would spring up out of nowhere, always leaving me disoriented, choking on the grains of fear.

I stuck it out as long as I could.

Meanwhile, back home, Mom quickly remarried—again. Her new husband owned a decent mobile home on the other side of Farmington. His last name was Jolly, and it seemed to suit him. For the first time in a long time, my mom was sober more than she was drunk.

Despite the fact that my new dad seemed better than the rest, I didn't have much faith in my mom's judgment when it came to men. So I elected to join my dad when he relocated to Durango, Colorado. A true blue-collar working man, Dad would rise before dawn, down a mug of black coffee and then be out the door. I wouldn't see him again until well after dark. Seven days a week, and even on Christmas.

Dad rarely spoke. And when he did have something to say, invariably it was to berate me for some mistake I may have made. Maybe I was the safest outlet for his life's frustrations, but whatever the reason, he focused on the negative—always.

In time, Dad's silence and criticisms grew deafening. I felt out of place in his home, even though I tried to make myself useful. I'd cook

T-bone steaks and potatoes some evenings and have it waiting on him when he trudged through the door. I'd do my best to keep the house clean and tidy, the way Mom had taught me to do it. But nothing ever seemed to please him. And I was tired of being his target.

School in Durango was tough. On foot, I'd have to go through deep snow to get to school every day. I was torn between two lifestyles that were both pretty miserable. But with my mom, at least there was that occasional glimmer of hope—that love that I longed for—especially when she was sober. "Why are you so smart, Jimbo?" I never answered her, but that secret knowledge that she saw something special in me fueled my drive to make something of myself.

Looking back now, I realize how important that message was to me. I clung to that token of hope that I had something of worth to offer. In those few words, she managed to convince me I could make things better for all of us. *I'm the smart one. It's up to me to fix it all.*

While mom had always slipped me as much money as she thought she could spare, dad was tight—real tight. I knew better than to expect any handouts from him, even for essentials.

One day he gave me money to get a haircut. I walked all the way into town, visited the local barber and skipped out without paying. Then I raced home to brag about what I'd done.

"No way could that guy catch me," I said, laughing. "I was out of there before he knew what was happening."

Dad didn't react the way I had expected. Instead of being proud, he slapped me hard across the face. I was stunned. My face burned with heat.

"Nobody likes a thief or a liar," he said, sternly. "You're gonna go back and pay that man his money. And you'll apologize to him, too."

I've never been more ashamed in my life. The weight of disappointing my dad was crushing to me. I already felt like he only tolerated me out of obligation. Now I'd gone and proven him right. I may have been smart, as Mom believed, but according to every adult I'd ever known, I was a problem also. And, sadly, that included my dad.

Aside from the incessant cold, I have few memories of school in Durango. I do, however, remember the gangly Mexican kid who was always goading me with threats that he'd beat me to a pulp. Since he was older and bigger, I believed him.

One afternoon, my brother Bobby was driving through town with me and I said, "Hey, there's that kid who wants to beat me up."

Bobby jerked the wheel to the side of the road and turned off the ignition. He got out of the car and said, "Hey! I hear you want to fight my brother. Why don't you fight me instead? I'm more your size."

"No, I don't want to fight you," said the kid, backing up and glaring at me.

Feeling bolder since my brother was with me, "Fine," I said. "I'll fight you."

The kid eyed Bobby. "You're gonna jump in, aren't you?"

"Nope," he said. "It's your fight."

I couldn't believe my brother was serious. He'd called my bluff!

There was no backing down now. I hit the guy with two swift successive punches like I'd learned at the Boys Club.

Bobby stood on the periphery, staring at us. *Surely this time he'll jump in*, I thought. The bully, almost a head taller than me, connected with a right hook, busted both my lips and knocked me down.

Not long after that skirmish, Dad returned from gathering wood for the potbellied stove. Vigorously stomping the snow off his boots, he came into the cabin looking even more stern than usual. "I talked to your mother today," he said. "I think it's best you go back and live with her. It's not working out here."

I froze in my tracks. I knew nothing I said would change his mind, so I stayed silent and bit back the tears.

Sure enough, before the spring thaw, I was back in Farmington.

Takeaways

- Trouble will find us wherever we go.
- Some people will try to break us down.
- Others will try to elevate us.
- Others will stay neutral and watch as we're being attacked.
- The trick is learning who is on your side in life and who is against you.

INGREDIENT #3

TURBULENCE CAN BE LIFE'S WAY OF SAYING IT'S TIME TO MOVE

B ack in Farmington with Mom and Mr. Jolly, I resumed my
training at the Boys Club and began fighting in matches. The
thing with boxing is you either get good fast, or you keep getting your butt kicked.

I fought with a fury, winning the majority of my fights in the light-
weight class. I loved the adrenaline high I got whenever the referee
raised my arm in the air and declared me the winner. I craved that
feeling more than anything I'd ever known. Boxing was the first thing
I'd ever succeeded at. Now that I had a taste of what it felt like to be a
winner, I wanted more!

But then the headaches started coming with a vengeance. The doctor
diagnosed them as a result of multiple concussions, linking them to an
accident I'd experienced at the age of six when my father wrecked his
dump truck. The truck had flipped over and over, as I was shot around
the cab like a pinball. Following the accident, I was in a coma for nine
hours.

While that certainly could have been the cause of the brain injuries,
Mom never told the doctor about all the men in her life who had beaten
me as a child.

"No more fights," the doctor warned. "It could be dangerous if he keeps getting hit in the head."

That was the last thing I wanted to hear as a teenager just starting to feel my oats. I'd found my own addiction: the thrill of winning. And now it was being stripped from me.

Boxing had given me confidence and a steady girlfriend—a petite, bubbly blonde named Janet, whose family had been rooted in Farmington for generations. She seemed like a nice girl from a good family. And with Janet on my arm I wasn't gripped by paralyzing fear anymore. I walked the school halls with my head held high. Still, there was always somebody wanting to fight me—the football jocks, the Mexicans, the cowboys. But I was good at boxing by then. I may have been forbidden from entering the ring, but I got in more than a dozen schoolyard fights and won them all.

My burly gym teacher wasn't pleased about this. "You better cool your jets, Markham," he said, throwing me against the locker.

Before I knew what had happened, I'd flipped him. I stood over him, glaring and breathing hard. I was sick and tired of grown men bullying me. I wasn't going to take it anymore.

He dusted himself off and marched me straight to the principal's office.

The principal peered at me with a hard stare. "You're never going to amount to anything, boy. You've got a choice: Leave town now, or I'm sending you to reform school."

Mom and I both knew reform school hadn't been a good option for my father. She made the long-distance call to her sister Lucille in Oklahoma, and I was shipped off once again.

Of all mom's siblings, my aunt was the only one who wasn't a drinker. Like my maternal grandparents, my aunt and her husband were devout, churchgoing folk, attending services every time the doors were opened—twice on Sunday and again on Wednesday nights. Instrumental music, dancing, and alcohol were all strictly forbidden. They owned a laundromat and turned in early every night.

My aunt and uncle had two kids of their own. While it may have seemed a good solution to send me to their home, I once again had that familiar feeling of being an outsider left to my own devices.

I was finishing out my ninth-grade school year in Oklahoma. When I returned home, Aunt Lucille was standing with the phone receiver in hand. "Jim, there's a girl from Farmington asking for you."

I took the phone and heard the soft voice of my girlfriend, Janet, from New Mexico.

"Hello, Jim," she said, a heavy sense of worry in her tone.

My heart skipped a beat as she hesitated.

"I'm pregnant."

The room began to spin. *Pregnant? Did she say pregnant?*

"When's the baby due?" I asked, as I paced the floor.

"The doctor says around Thanksgiving."

"Is it. . . are you saying. . ." The words failed me.

"Yes, Jim," Janet said softly. "It's yours. Ours. The baby is ours."

I stood confused and almost in shock, but in a strange way, also happy.

"We'll be ready by then," I assured her. "I promise."

I hung up the receiver slowly, in complete shock. I felt dizzy, like I had all those times when I'd gotten my bell rung in a fight. My ears were ringing, my heart was pounding out of my chest. *I'm 15! I don't know a thing about being a father. Now I've got to figure out how to take care of Janet and a child—and myself.*

Aunt Lucille finished drying the dishes and then put her hands on her ample hips. "What have you gotten yourself into now, Jim?" Her lips pursed in disapproval.

I didn't care what anybody else thought—certainly not Aunt Lucille. But something about the way she was looking at me with such disgust—like she could see my whole doomed future ahead of me—flipped a switch in my brain.

What a minute. I've always wanted to belong. The timing was far from ideal, but I decided that good would come of it somehow. I would step up to the plate and be a real man by building the family I'd always wanted! And I certainly wouldn't repeat the mistakes my parents had made. Although I was scared out of my wits, Janet and our baby would feel loved and protected by me no matter what it took. I was determined to find a way to provide for them, to never abandon them.

Because Janet and I were only 15, our parents had to sign for us to get married. With her mom as a chaperone, we traveled to Texarkana, the closest place we could legally marry that young. Mom met us there, and we had a small ceremony.

Then my new bride and I returned to Farmington where Janet's family owned about a thousand acres of land. Her parents agreed to let us live there with them. I was surprised to get that kind of reception from her family after I'd gotten their teenage daughter pregnant.

Janet was the oldest of three. Her father was quiet and kind. He worked in the oil field and kept his head down. Her mother—a loud, petite redhead—ruled the roost. Like pretty much everybody in the entire town, they were Mormons. I appreciated the church's emphasis on family and how Janet's family, who'd been a part of the church for generations, embraced me as one of their own. I studied their faith and happily converted. As the son of an alcoholic, the church's strict rules on drinking and other vices made sense to me. The doctrine seemed to give me a clear-cut way to build a happy family, a plan I was determined to follow.

With a baby on the way, I decided there was no point in going back to school. Besides, all I had to show for the ninth grade was a failing report card. What I really needed was a job—and fast.

My wife's family stepped in to help with that, too. With Janet's family connections, I landed a job working as a parts chaser for the Ford dealership in town. The position suited me, as I'd always been interested in cars—maybe a little too interested. One day, I was hot-rodding the company truck through the middle of town, when I slid around a corner and suddenly came eyeball-to-eyeball with the company president. I'd come within a whisper of hitting him as he crossed the street.

Needless to say, that was the end of my job at Ford.

But I didn't know what to do. With a new baby on the way and no job, I was scared. More than scared, I was terrified.

That's when my mother gave me a rare piece of helpful advice: "Your uncle Clarence always did well as a barber," she calmly said.

Working as a barber sounded a lot better than working in oil fields like most of the men I knew, but the closest barber school was 500 miles away in Lubbock, Texas. I had to lie about my age to get in the school, which required that I be 16 years of age.

Janet and I moved to Lubbock. I pushed hard through the program, learning my new trade as fast as I could. I completed the six-month course in just three and a half months, passing both the written test and the practical, which required me to show my expertise by providing a haircut, a facial, and a shave. I passed!

Our daughter, who Janet decided to name Vickie, was born around Thanksgiving, before my 16th birthday. She was perfect with white blonde hair like her mother's. I loved her from the moment I laid eyes on her, and when she wrapped her tiny hand around my little finger, I was overjoyed.

After graduation, the school let me know about an opening with a barber shop in Carlsbad, New Mexico. Despite it being in the opposite corner of the state—again, 500 miles from Farmington—I took the job.

Soon, Janet and our infant daughter Vickie and I moved into a small apartment. We didn't know a soul in Carlsbad. My baby face revealed I was by far the youngest in the shop, and at only 16 years of age, I had trouble getting clients to trust me. Each day I woke up feeling panicked about my ability to support my family.

A month after I started, a barber I was working with killed his wife in a jealous rage. Then he shot himself. Cold fear gripped me when I heard the news of the murder-suicide. Supposedly, he'd caught her having an affair with a local police officer. I'd certainly seen my fair share of violent men in my life, but a murderer? *What on earth could make a guy do something like that? And if it could happen to someone I worked with, could it happen to my mother too?*

The shop owner insisted I move over and take the dead man's chair. And if that wasn't bad enough, the very same cop who'd supposedly been having the affair with the barber's wife had become my client. I had a hard time steadying my hands as I cut his hair.

I hung with the job for a few months, until a chair opened at Johnny's Barber Shop in Farmington. I continued studying the doctrines of the Mormon church and I became an Elder and started teaching Sunday school.

Eager to increase my earnings to support my family, I got straight to work, charging $1.50 for a regular haircut and $2 for flat tops. Shortly after I arrived, Johnny asked me to open up a new barber shop with the promise of selling it to me at a good price. I spent a whole year building up the clientele, and then he wanted to double the price he'd originally given me. Yet another broken promise.

I was ecstatic when my brother Bobby left the trucking business with my dad and moved to Farmington with his wife and kids. He'd gone to barber school and was working at a place across town. We agreed to pool our money together and open up Markham Barber Shop. Even though we had hardly ever lived under the same roof, I still longed to be close and was willing to do nearly anything to foster that relationship. Shortly before Thanksgiving, Janet announced that she was expecting again.

The birth of my son, Robert, followed in May. We agreed to call him Bobby, after my brother, and like his sister, he was another beautiful, fair-haired child. I was a 17-year-old father of two, and I was so happy to have a home to go to with a family I loved so completely.

Vickie had decided she was a daddy's girl. The first 10 months of her life, she'd fall asleep on my chest with her tiny hand resting on my chin. She toddled over to me every time I walked through the door and wrapped her little arms around my legs and held on tight. I was building the family I'd always longed for, and I was one very grateful young man.

I loved the way Vickie rained kisses on my cheek and the feel of Bobby snuggled safe in my arms as he slept.

While things were humming along at the barber shop, Janet soon became restless taking care of a toddler and a newborn at home. With all the hours I was putting in at the shop, I didn't have much time to help her with the kids. I'd watched my mother struggle financially all those years, and my priority was to serve as a good provider for my family, to never have to run in the middle of the night when rent came due or to make my wife wait tables for tips.

But Janet had always been strong-willed, and she frequently announced she was leaving me. There was nothing I dreaded more than the breakdown of my family. They were my reason for everything.

I focused on trying to keep the peace at any cost, even sleeping on a rollaway bed in the back room of the shop on many nights when she'd take the kids and go to her parents' place.

I was stumped. I had no idea how to mend fences with Janet. I was working as hard as I knew, following all the rules of the church, trying to do everything right, but once again, nothing I did seemed good enough. I took to sleeping on a cot at the shop for longer stretches at a time when Janet would go home with the children to her parents.

At this time, our shop was struggling, and my brother had grown tired of not making any money. "Dad's got a gig driving dump trucks in Texas," he said. "I think it's best if I move on and join him."

I didn't argue. There was no point. It was yet another disappointment that struck deep, but I kept my head up and stayed the course. My brother and I had only been in business together less than a year. I'd learned early that life doesn't always go as expected and that people can't always be who we want them to be. The trick was learning how to adapt to whatever new challenge came my way.

"I understand," I said, trying to hide my disappointment.

We shook hands, he picked up his belongings, and left town with his wife and kids. As much as I longed to be close to my brother, we were too different and had never really found a way to connect the way I'd hoped.

My new business partner, Bill Brenton, who came from Oklahoma and had his barber's license, brought a surge of energy into the place. He had come into our shop when he first got to town looking for a job. Of course, I couldn't hire him then. When he heard my brother left, he came in and asked for his chair. We really complemented each other. Before long, we'd built the shop up to be one of the busiest in town.

Although I was introverted by nature, I'd come to learn from Bill, who was a decade older, that the friendlier I was with customers, the more likely they were going to become regulars.

One of my first regulars was an old veteran with a wooden leg who started coming in every day. He'd sit in a chair at the back of the shop with his checkerboard from early morning until closing each night. An Alabama native, he taught me to play checkers and helped me pass the time when business was slow.

When I got the hang of the game, I spent every spare moment trying to improve my skills. I discovered having a good strategy in place rather than being guided by emotions could make all the difference. I came to favor a strategy called the "old fourteenth," which calls for going straight down the middle against your opponent. I became obsessed, and toward the end of our first year in business, I'd started beating the old man more often than not.

One afternoon, he broke the news he was going back home to Alabama. We played one last game. I won. I always wondered if he let me win.

"You're one lucky son of a gun," said the old man, winking at me. The student had become the teacher.

I got the feeling he somehow saw the same deep loneliness in me that he saw in himself. We shook hands, and I hated to see him go.

Before he hobbled out the door, he insisted on leaving his checkerboard behind. "This one belongs here with you, Jim," he said. "I'll pick up another one when I get where I'm going."

One of my customers, who was a regular, invited me to go up in his private plane. Excited, I met him early one morning at the airfield. Soon we were up soaring over the oilfields, mesas, and arroyos. Short of becoming a father, I'd never experienced such a rush. It felt magical to suddenly see everything from a different point of view. I quickly became intrigued by the process of piloting a plane.

"You know, Jim, it's pretty easy to become a pilot," he said. "With all the questions you're asking, I have a feeling you'd be good at it."

Once we landed, he told me everything I'd need to do if I wanted to become a pilot. I immediately got a book and studied all the rules and regulations with as much intensity as I'd committed to becoming a barber. I soon acquired 40 hours of flying time and passed both the practical and written exams. Shortly after my 18th birthday, I earned my private pilot's license. From that moment on, I flew every chance I could get. There, high above the earth, I felt some sense of control that I'd never known before.

When I was flying, I rarely hit turbulence. My marriage. . . that was a completely different story.

With each separation, she'd announce she was leaving, clear everything out of our small house, and take the kids and go home to her mother. My son Bobby had become a papa's boy. He'd be sobbing every time and begging, "Please, please, Daddy don't leave. Let me stay with you."

It was heartbreaking.

Often during those separation periods, I'd see her out on the main drag chatting up guys, or worse, sitting in a car with one at the A&W drive-in.

The thought hit me hard: *I've married my mother.* Eventually, I finally accepted the truth of the situation. The idyllic home life I'd dreamt of was never going to happen—at least not with Janet. Neither of us were mature enough to pull together in a healthy way and save our marriage. I grew tired of being left alone again and again.

By age 19, I was the divorced father of two children and alone again.

Takeaways

- You're likely to experience some failures before you start chalking up wins. That's okay. You're training for your breakthrough moment.

- Having a good strategy in place is better than going off emotions.

- Life doesn't always go as expected. The trick is adapting to whatever new challenge it throws your way.

- Teamwork takes TWO people working together to reach the same goal.

- If your partner isn't moving in the same direction as you, you'll just spin in circles and never reach the goal you're aiming for. . . whether that's a successful business or a happy family.

INGREDIENT #4

WHEN YOU
GET A SHOT, TAKE IT

T he majority of my clientele were Mormons. In the wake of the divorce, I lost not only my family and my church, but about half of my business—a grief that compounded the heartbreak of my failed marriage. Once again, I was an outsider.

In order to cope with the pain and anxiety from such rejection, I worked even harder than before.

My new partner Bill and I each had our strong suits. Bill, gregarious and funny, got a lot of clients. Everybody liked him, and he did good work, too. I was quieter and somewhat reserved, but I was stronger as a barber technically.

To excel, I needed to put more effort into developing my people skills. If I could teach myself how to fly a plane, I figured I could learn how to be more like Bill. My strategy was to observe, absorb, digest, and then create my own spin on the social skills that seemed to come so naturally to him.

I devoured books like Dale Carnegie's *How to Win Friends and Influence People*, *The Power of Positive Thinking* by Napoleon Hill, and *Think and Grow Rich* by Norman Vincent Peale. I'd never been much of a reader, but studying books to become a barber and a pilot had worked out well for me, and those three titles had struck a chord: I wanted to win more customers. I wanted to be happier. And I certainly wanted more money.

Six months passed, and the shop was starting to take off. I began making deposits at the bank across the street where one of the tellers, Lena, always greeted me with a big, friendly smile. She was one of the prettiest girls in town, so I made a point of getting in her line each day. Within three months, we were hitched. With the new social skills I'd acquired from reading self-help books and observing Bill's charming ways, I was determined to make this marriage a success, just as we'd done with the business.

Bill matched my enthusiasm and love for the barber shop. He was always pushing to make our business better and was full of ideas about how to make that happen. Soon, he suggested we attend the Roffler Training Academy.

In those days, Roffler was the only company teaching men's hair cutting and styling in the US. Its technique was based on a European style of razor cutting that was the hottest thing going, but I was hesitant to waste the money on the training and reluctant to leave my new wife.

"We could charge more money if we had some new skills," Bill argued. "I'm going. You in or out?"

Bill knew I couldn't let anyone get a leg up on me, and I knew he was right about needing to stay on the cutting edge of the industry. Besides, I loved learning new skills and had always been eager to tackle a challenge. I'd always gained confidence by diving in and doing my best.

"Okay, I'm in," I said it, hesitant, because I knew $350 in expenses was a lot of money. But, nevertheless, I was off to Tyler, Texas, determined to succeed.

Bill and I both graduated as stars of the class. Once certified, we advertised our shop as the first in New Mexico to have this new and improved method of cutting hair. We also raised our rates. Finally, I had a partner I could count on.

Roffler was expanding by using distributors to teach their technique. The new distributor for New Mexico noticed my eagerness to excel and told me for each person I got to sign up for the course at $350, he'd pay me $100. We shook hands on it, and I got five stylists to sign up. I had big plans for that $500 commission.

But he never honored the deal, and I never saw my cut.

I was livid. My dad was right. *Nobody likes a liar or a cheat.* I'd learned the hard way the importance of a man's word. I'd also learned that trust was something to be earned.

Three months later, Bill and I competed at the Texas State Razor-Cutting Championship in Dallas. More than 700 people in the industry were milling about, watching the barbers competing. As first-time attendees, we were there to learn. We didn't place in the competition, but we wandered around studying what the winners had done, making mental notes about the techniques and styles that most appealed to the judges.

The first Roffler Razor-Cutting National Championship was slated to be held that very afternoon in the same complex. With nothing to lose, Bill and I both entered the final competition. Then we quickly scoured the streets, each looking for a model to fill our chairs. Not surprisingly, we had no luck convincing strangers to let us cut their hair, so just as the championship competition was about to start, Bill agreed to step in as my model. I couldn't return the favor. The morning's winners had all styled dark-haired models, so we both suspected my fair hair wouldn't show as well as his.

We'd also observed that the judges preferred a smooth and shiny finish compared to the natural look we'd used in the competition that morning. I adjusted accordingly. Every detail counted. With the mental focus of a pilot before takeoff, I ran through the checklist knowing there'd be no room for error.

That afternoon as I stood behind the chair in the cavernous convention center, I was determined to apply everything I'd seen the winners do. The hitch was that Bill's dark hair was extremely fine. I was in the middle of the repetitive comb-razor, comb-razor, comb-razor technique when disaster struck. My hands, shaking from nerves, caused the razor to slip, leaving a gaping hole in the crown of his hair.

Just then, the words from my old boxing coach resurfaced: *Don't give up. You're never beaten until you quit.* I kept working to camouflage my mistakes, giving Bill the shiniest, smoothest finish I could possibly achieve.

When it came time to announce the winners, I patted Bill on the shoulder and said, "Well, I gave it my best shot."

Then the announcer teased the crowd with a dramatic pause before announcing first place, "And the grand champion is. . . Number 14!"

We cheered again, as I looked around for the big winner.

"Markham!" Bill shouted, shaking me by the arm. "That's you! You won, Markham!"

When the shock settled, I walked to the winner's circle, incredulous. I was a winner. And not just a winner. . . the grand champion!

Just as it had with boxing, that first victory lit a fire in me. I entered every contest I could find. I'd work all day, and then after closing time at the shop, I'd practice three nights a week for two hours at a time on various models, determined to hone my craft. I plucked stray hairs above the brow and made sure the lines around the ears and the neckline were crisp. I wielded a dark eyebrow pencil like an artist diving into a fresh canvas—filling in any weak areas that caught my eye. I also perfected my blow-drying technique to get that glossy finish the judges preferred. For competitions, I'd add makeup to my model's neck, color his hair blue-black, and require that he wear a tuxedo.

Soon, I was winning every contest I entered. I racked up awards all across the Southwest and as far east as Pittsburgh. Then came the Hair Olympics in Cincinnati. I put myself into intense training, knowing I'd be competing against the best barbers in the country—men with far more experience then I'd gained in my short years.

But just as I was beginning to soar, I made a big mistake. The night before the competition, I decided to go out drinking with another young friend. We wound up staying out way too late, and when it was time to compete the next morning, my hands were shaking. *You deserve to lose,* I thought, kicking myself for breaking my own rule about being prepared. Despite fighting a raging hangover, I won the silver medal, but I felt incredibly disappointed in myself for not earning gold. I vowed to never pull a stunt like that again. Lesson learned.

A week later, during a break at my barber shop, I opened up a *Playboy* magazine and I read an interview with Jay Sebring, a hair stylist to the biggest male stars in Hollywood. The article reported he was charging $50 for a cut.

What the heck? I'm a national champion and I'm lucky if I get $5, which is still double what anybody else is charging. This guy is getting 10 times what I make?

I looked around my shop, thinking about what kind of luck a man like Jay Sebring must have. But then I had another thought. If that kind of success could happen for Jay Sebring, why couldn't it happen for me too?

It was a ridiculous thought. And as soon as it surfaced, so did all those old criticisms from my past: My principal telling me I'd never amount to anything. My father never uttering a single kind word to me. My mother choosing her abusive husbands over me.

But I couldn't help but wonder what might happen if I dared to silence all those negative voices in my head.

At age 23, I was becoming my own man. In that moment, I made an intentional choice—I could believe I'd never amount to anything and prove them all right, or I could believe I'd been born to win and set out to prove them all wrong.

With the magazine still in hand, I picked up the phone and called Sebring International in Los Angeles. Full of the hard-won confidence I'd gained from my year-long winning streak, I gave Jay Sebring my spiel: "I heard you have a line of products, and I'd be interested in helping you distribute them here in New Mexico." Then I took it one step further, following a nudge about what might really strike his interest. "I also read that you have a special technique for cutting hair. I'm the National Men's Razor Cutting Champion and a medalist in the Hair Olympics. If my technique is better than yours, we can use mine going forward."

It was a risky move, but I figured this might be my one shot to learn from the best in the business. I didn't have anything to lose.

I waited through a long silence from the other end of the line.

"You sound awfully sure of yourself," Jay said. "I'm intrigued. Why don't you come out here and we'll see who has the best technique? It will cost you $1,000 to observe me work. Then, if you're interested in opening a Sebring franchised shop, you can apply that $1,000 toward the $10,000 fee to do so."

"And if I win?" I asked, sensing he had a competitive streak like me.

"If you win, you don't owe me anything."

I smiled. "You're on."

I borrowed the $1,000 that Jay requested as earnest money and flew to LA that very weekend. The day of our match, when I arrived at Sebring International, I realized the photos in the magazine hadn't done his shop justice. I'd barely traveled out of the southwest and Texas. I'd never seen any shop quite like this. I was in awe.

The salon occupied prime space on Melrose and Fairfax in West Hollywood, convenient for the many celebrities he served. It was the epicenter of the industry at this time. The walls—all chrome and mirrors—were studded with portraits of Hollywood's most celebrated tough guys: Steve McQueen, Paul Newman, Kirk Douglas, Henry Fonda, Marlon Brando—and, yes, *Ol' Blue Eyes*—Frank Sinatra.

I steadied my nerves by taking in every detail. I counted 17 stylists — two-thirds of them women—working on customers, virtually all male. Although a lot of the clientele were entertainers, many were just leaders of industry, lawyers, doctors—anyone who was important. Every chair was occupied and the place was kept spotless. Mellow jazz music played from corner speakers, yet the vibe in the room was high energy and creative. What struck me the most was the air of professionalism. Every aspect of the salon seemed carefully controlled—as precise as the cuts Jay gave—rather than the chaos typically found in most shops.

It was clear: Jay ran a serious business.

Within minutes of my arrival, the receptionist escorted me up a flight of stairs to Jay's private office. "This is where he cuts and styles his most elite clientele," she explained. At that moment, I sensed something special was about to happen.

We entered to find Jay sitting at his oversized desk. Ten years older than me, Jay stood to greet me, dismissing his receptionist with a kind offer of thanks.

Dressed in his signature hip-huggers—maroon, and matching short-sleeved shirt—he made quite an impression. His shoes coordinated with his belt, and although he was smaller than I expected, his larger-than-life presence dominated his private lair, perhaps because his dramatic mane of thick, dark hair fell perfectly layered, centered by his warm, brown eyes.

Jay quickly laid out the rules, introducing me to Hollywood icon Van Johnson. "My brave friend has agreed to be our model today," Jay said with a smile. "You'll cut one side of his hair, and I'll do the other. You can select which side you'd prefer to style, then we'll figure out who has the best cutting technique."

I had to admit, I was a little nervous. One of MGM's biggest matinee idols, Van Johnson, who had starred in many movies I loved as a boy was sitting in the chair and I was about to cut his hair. A wave of apprehension came over me as I shook the movie star's hand.

Jay's tools were shears, combs, and a black blow dryer. They were laid out on a narrow table.

As soon as the shampoo girl finished her job, Van settled into a black styling chair, fidgeting with unease. He trusted Jay, but putting his hair in the hands of a young, new stylist was a real leap of faith.

I picked up on Van's nervous energy, which added to the pressure I already felt. A lot was at stake, but I gave it my all, and by the time I'd finished with the blow dryer I was satisfied with my performance. His medium-blonde hair was now full on the sides, but thinner and shorter on top, and his neckline appeared natural in the back.

"That's the best razor work I've ever seen," Jay said, making me feel like the only person in the room.

Then Jay went to work, using straight shears for most of the cut and then finishing with the blending shears. I had never seen anyone do that before. I'd only seen clippers, razors, or straight shears. For the next 30 minutes I scrutinized his every move, asking questions intermittently. He was quiet and focused as he worked. He'd step back occasionally to look at the natural movement of the hair. He, too, finished with a quick blow dry.

As soon as I saw what he'd done, I recognized that his way—cutting shape into the hair and following its natural growth pattern—was revolutionary. There was no hype here. He had beaten me fair and square.

This was one contest I didn't mind losing, because Jay had something to teach me. I paid Jay the agreed-upon $1,000 that day and signed a note for an additional $9,000 franchise fee plus 6 percent of sales. That was a big sum of money, but I believed my investment would pay off. "You'll have the first franchised Sebring International shop," Jay said, congratulating me and shaking my hand.

Takeaways

- Decide what you want to do, and then go after it with all you've got.
- You may have to face a steep learning curve. Keep going.
- Losing is easy. Winning takes effort.
- Never give up. You're never beaten until you quit.
- No one likes a thief or a liar.
- We must dare to bet on ourselves.
- Remain humble and admit when someone else's way is better.
- One brave move can propel us forward, even if it's in a way we don't expect.

THE ROAD BEHIND YOU DOES NOT DEFINE THE ROAD AHEAD

When I arrived in Hollywood to meet with Jay, I wasted zero mental energy on being insecure about my New Mexico accent or my lack of education. None of that mattered. The only thing that mattered was how I handled myself going forward. Within a month after I'd signed the IOU, my partner Bill and I had sold Markham Barber Shop in Farmington and opened Sebring International on Menaul Boulevard. The new location was centered in Albuquerque's Northeast Heights—an area of nice neighborhoods at the base of the Sandia Mountains.

Money was tight, but we built out the space to look as much like the original Sebring International, as possible. We put in black-and-white linoleum squares like a checkerboard. We installed pecky cedar wood planking on the front of the building and put the name "Sebring International" in custom lettering on the wood. We installed bunk beds in the back room where we slept during the week, going home to Farmington only on the weekends. We made the stations and reception area look the same as Sebring's.

My pregnant wife Lena wasn't happy about my decision to open a shop in Albuquerque, but I wanted to build a better life than the one we had in Farmington. Albuquerque was the largest city in New Mexico, and the opportunities there seemed endless.

"Once we get the shop rolling, I'll buy a house for us," I promised, eager to make my second wife happy.

Our clients weren't celebrities, but I wanted to make them feel like stars. I flew out to LA several times for intensive training with Jay. I was a sponge and I soaked up everything I could about his cutting and styling techniques. He showed patience, as I peppered my mentor with endless questions about what he was doing and why.

I knew from reading that original magazine article that Jay had a reputation for living a high-octane life—studying martial arts with Bruce Lee and racing cars with Steve McQueen. Considering he took his name from the Sebring International Raceway, I'd expected him to live in the fast lane. But I quickly realized his celebrity life included a party scene that took excess to a level I could never have imagined. In addition to his late nights and luxury cars, every few weeks he flew to Las Vegas to cut the hair of Frank Sinatra, Paul Anka, and Sammy Davis, Jr. This also included several casino owners.

One evening, after putting in a full day's work cutting clients with me in his private office, he said, "C'mon, Markham. Let's head out."

Jay offered to let me crash at his pad, a Bavarian-style home with a dark history in Benedict Canyon. He gave me a quick tour, explaining that actress Jean Harlow had once owned it, but her producer husband Paul Bern had blown his brains out upstairs in the bedroom after only two months of marriage. Then he lowered his voice to a near whisper and said, "This place is haunted."

At that moment, an apparition emerged from Jay's bedroom upstairs—an angel with big doe eyes and long, blonde hair. Barefooted, she padded across the shag carpet. "Hello, I'm Sharon," she said, extending her hand with a vibe of vulnerability and shyness about her.

Initially, I mistook her for a teenager, but then I recognized her as Sharon Tate, the star of *Valley of the Dolls*.

"Sharon popped by for a visit," Jay said. "She and her husband Roman Polanski have rented a place in Beverly Hills not too far from here."

I knew who she was, and I also knew that Jay had a history with her. She'd actually lived in this house with Jay for a couple years before she married the famous director.

The daughter of a US Army colonel, she was an Army Brat—and a very beautiful one.

Jay announced the three of us would be visiting his favorite haunt that night, a private club called The Candy Store in Beverly Hills, "Where all the beautiful people hang out."

I was in awe the first night I accompanied Jay to The Candy Store. Making our way through a throng of people waiting behind the velvet ropes to gain entry, men had to be members or the guest of a member; women merely had to be judged pretty enough by the doorman. This crowd stood in sharp contrast to the hippies I'd seen on the Sunset Strip. Here, the women wore chic minis with high heels or go-go boots, and the men dressed in stylish suits.

The doorman motioned us to the front of the line. Jay casually said, "This is my guest, Jim Markham. He's with us."

"Yes, sir, Mr. Sebring." The bouncer tipped his hat to me with respect.

Once inside, I took in everything as Jay filled me in. Herb Alpert, Paul Newman, Steve McQueen—they were all either part owners or members of the place. He explained. "They even own a piece of my business."

This surprised me. I made a mental note: *Investing in a hair stylist. Hmm.*

Like many of the men in the club, Jay was dressed in a dark Italian suit. I'd worn my sharpest-looking sportscoat with a coordinated shirt and jeans, but it worked. The bar stood to the left with about two dozen people crowded around it, including some of Hollywood's biggest names. It seemed everyone in The Candy Store was connected to the entertainment industry one way or another.

A small dance floor to the right of the bar was so packed you couldn't see where it ended. The other half of the place consisted of small tables—most of them occupied. We'd barely made it through the entry when Peter Lawford motioned for us to join him. The actor, magnetic and strikingly handsome, was surrounded by some of the most beautiful women I'd ever seen. We slid into his booth, as they all made room for us.

No one could hear much of anything over the music and I was grateful not to have to make idle chit-chat. I kept my mouth shut and observed, studying Jay's easy manner. Women flocked around him almost as much as they did Peter Lawford, whose famous head of hair was another that Sebring styled.

I was just beginning to relax and enjoy being treated as an insider for once. A buxom brunette sidled up to me, chatting away. When Tom Jones jumped up on a nearby table and started belting out his latest hit, most of the women in the place—including the brunette—immediately ran to surround him. It felt like a scene out of an Elvis movie that Lena loved.

"Welcome to Hollywood's British Invasion," Jay laughed with a shrug. "You win some; you lose some."

Later, in the wee hours as we were waiting for the valet to bring his Porsche around, Jay stopped, looked me square in the eye and said, "You remind me so much of myself at your age. If anything were to ever happen, I'd want you to take over for me, because you're really the only one I know who understands the technique."

Taken aback, I couldn't find the words to reply. I was just getting to know him, and this level of trust was unexpected.

Meeting Jay Sebring had felt like a godsend to me from the start. I was hungry for something more and Jay responded to that drive. He became my creative mentor and my friend. He not only opened my eyes to a world I never dreamt existed, he took an interest in my career and recognized my talent and ambition. After I became his first franchisee and the distributor of his line of hair care products, Jay adopted me as his protégé.

I was happy to be in his orbit.

He had a successful formula in terms of his shop, and I wanted to capture that mystique as his first franchisee. But what had me even more interested (from my encounter earlier in my career with the Roffler distributor) was the idea of convincing other barbers and stylists to carry Sebring products. At the time, hair care products were being sold primarily in drugstores and in supermarkets. I saw a huge opportunity to create a new distribution channel.

For my plan to work, I needed to teach professionals the Sebring technique of cutting and styling, but also teach them daily washing with our products. This new concept for men, who at the time only shampooed maybe once a week and used Brylcreem, was a game-changer and I knew it. It was a revolutionary new idea.

Jay and I talked about taking his products directly to hair care professionals in New Mexico, Texas, Arizona, and Colorado. Until then, he'd been exclusively selling his line by doing special events at high-end department stores, where he'd talk about his philosophy while demonstrating his technique and products. He hadn't yet considered signing on professionals to retail those products to their customers for at-home use.

I convinced him there was a lot of money to be made in distributing his products this way. He loved my ideas and gave me the green light to be his distributor in all four states.

Going all in, I'd fly my plane from town to town and scan the Yellow Pages to figure out the best barber in each area. Then I'd cold-call and try to convince them to let me do a demo. I was confident that if I could show the Sebring technique to these key barbers, then I could convince them to become distributors. They'd retail the product to their customers and certify other shops and barbers to sell in their area too.

In Albuquerque, I was convinced I'd convert everyone in town to Sebring; I was on fire. Full of determination, I hosted a presentation and told the barbers in attendance all about why Sebring's way was so much better than anything they'd been doing and why they needed to sign up immediately. Not a single barber agreed to become a Sebring-certified shop.

But I refused to quit.

Next stop, El Paso. I had a buddy there and we stayed out partying all night. The following morning, I felt terrible. My head was pounding, and I seriously considered canceling the entire event. But the barber I'd contacted there had gathered 15 other barbers to hear my presentation and I couldn't let him down.

I went on with the presentation as planned, even though I was fighting one of the worst hangovers ever. Dehydrated and fatigued, I couldn't muster up my usual bravado. I was quiet and listened to their questions instead of talking over them, as I do sometimes. I answered in a soft voice—not out of respect, but because I was feeling like my head was about to explode. It was a lesson I should've learned long ago, but sometimes it takes a little time to finally change your ways.

All 15 barbers signed on to become Sebring-certified shops that day. By sheer accident, I'd learned an important lesson about salesmanship: *Nobody likes to have something crammed down their throat.* If I'd been feeling better, I'd have blasted in that morning with too much enthusiasm, too eager to make a sale, and I may have even come off as a know-it-all—convinced my way was better than theirs. But because of the hangover, I was slower, calmer, less aggressive. I was able to quietly demonstrate the method and then help them understand how becoming a Sebring shop would benefit each of them.

It worked!

Ironically, not long after that, I got a chance to do a demo with Johnny Tafoya, the barber in Farmington who'd first trained me to do flat tops. He recruited 10 other barbers to come to my presentation. All of them signed on, and Johnny became a Sebring-certified shop in the town.

I was on a roll, and Jay was pleased. He knew that having proof of concept with Sebring International in Albuquerque was vital to our shared future, so he made himself readily available to me as I was learning the ropes. I stayed in almost daily contact with him for the first few months. He proved to be an excellent mentor, patient and encouraging at every step, insisting that the difference between a good cut and a great cut all came down to the minor details.

Jay finally flew in, and I laid the groundwork to get him a ton of publicity. A local reporter wrote a feature about Jay in *The Albuquerque Journal*. Radio stations aired interviews with the "highest paid men's stylist in the nation," and all the local TV news outlets ran a segment about the legendary *stylist to the stars.*

Eager to show Jay a good time in my town, I wined and dined him.

One night, I took him to a club. Within a few minutes, a bevy of beauties were hanging around our table, just as they did in Los Angeles. No matter where we went, people were drawn to Jay. His charm was magnetic.

The next week, I got a call from Stretch "Captain Billy" Scherer, who'd read about us in the paper. He hosted a popular children's morning show on Channel 13 that competed with *Captain Kangaroo*.

"I hear you got a good cutting style going on," he said. "Tell you what. I'll let you cut my hair. If you do a good job, I'll tell everybody in town. If you do a bad job, I'll tell everybody in town."

"Sounds good to me," I said, with more confidence than I felt. I was still learning Jay's technique. Stretch was popular and often emceed charity events and fashion shows. He really did seem to know everybody, and the stakes were high.

Stretch came in and I grew even more worried. His hair was wiry and tough to control. If I cut it using Jay's technique, it might end up sticking out all over his head like a baby bird's. I took a deep breath and decided to do my best to apply the skills Jay had taught me, but I also improvised.

When I finally finished blow drying his hair, I was as surprised as he appeared to be. "I love it," he said, admiring his reflection. "It's the best cut I've ever had."

True to his word, he talked me up in an interview he gave to *The Albuquerque Journal*, and mentioned me in radio and TV appearances. Needless to say, I got an avalanche of publicity. And within a few weeks of opening our doors, our profits soared. I hired more stylists and they all booked up right away, too.

Meanwhile, Lena had joined me in Albuquerque and given birth to our son. He was a beautiful boy, blonde like his older half-siblings, and looked like his mother. We named him James Jay and decided to call him Jay, an honor that pleased my mentor tremendously.

Unfortunately, our son's name was one of the last things my wife Lena and I agreed on. One weekend when Jay was barely nine months old, Lena announced, "Listen, Jim. I'm taking Jay on the bus to Farmington to visit my friend Sandy and her husband. I'll be staying at a motel. We'll be back late tomorrow. Can you drop us off at the bus station on your way to the shop?"

"Sure," I said. She gave me a peck on the cheek, and I noticed that she'd carefully done her makeup.

Something didn't feel right. I got suspicious. When I got home from work, I called every motel in town and asked if Lena Markham was registered there. No dice.

When she came home with our son late the next day, I confronted her. Finally, she broke down crying and admitted that she left Jay with her friend while she spent the night with another man. "All you do is work, and I'm stuck here with the baby all day," she said.

I was boiling inside, but I held my temper and my tongue. There was just no point in arguing. I'd made up my mind.

The next morning, I put her and our son on a bus back to her small town of Snyder, Texas. One of my clients was a lawyer and he helped me file for divorce. It was finalized a month later.

So, despite wanting so wholeheartedly to have a healthy family to call my own, I was still too young to make it work. Or maybe it was because most of my male role models had been terribly flawed, and I had no clue how to be a good husband. Or maybe I wasn't really such a bad husband, but I hadn't found the right partner. Whatever the reason, it seemed I'd married my mother not once, but twice, and I was beginning to think no one would ever stay true.

My response to this latest betrayal was the same as before. I poured everything I had into making my business a success, and my efforts were rewarded with great success.

Sometime in the middle of July, I decided to fly up to Los Angeles to surprise Jay. I found him in his office, where Sharon was once again hanging out. Now in the last trimester of her first pregnancy and all aglow, she welcomed me with a gentle kiss on the cheek.

In Jay's chair sat Steve McQueen. Jay reintroduced us, telling the actor that I shared their love of fast cars and motorcycles.

I took note of the way Jay so smoothly found a way to work into the conversation a common interest I shared with Steve. If I was going to hang in these circles, I couldn't afford to be intimidated and hang back. I thought about what I learned from Dale Carnegie: *To be interesting, you have to be interested.*

Steve puffed a cigarette while admiring himself in the mirror. "Jay, I liked the look you gave me for *The Thomas Crown Affair*. I want to stay in that lane for a while."

Known as the "King of Cool" as well as for his hot temper with producers and directors, the anti-hero star of such hits as *The Great Escape*, *Bullitt*, and *The Magnificent Seven* was notoriously prickly. But his relationship with Jay went beyond the shop and had evolved into a genuine friendship.

As the conversation continued, we talked about everything including the two men's service in the military. Steve had joined the Merchant Marines while Jay had served in the Navy during the Korean War and first learned to cut hair during his time at sea. Despite their stylish appearances, both were tough guys who thrived on adrenaline-inducing pursuits and had an eye for the ladies.

I quickly learned that Steve smoked pot on a daily basis. Then Jay shrugged his shoulders and said, "Now I do it to come down from cocaine."

"Cocaine?" I asked.

"Yeah, it's all the rage," Jay said. "Gives you a big energy boost; it's not addictive."

I'd wondered how Jay managed to work at his shop all day and then hang out with his famous clients until the wee hours every morning. Now I knew his secret!

Sharon stood up, cradled her belly protectively and said, "I think I'll head back up the canyon to my place. Come by later; bring Jim if you like."

She kissed Jay on the lips.

"Sure, love," said Jay, winking.

It was well after midnight when Jay and I drove up the canyon toward the estate that Roman Polanski and Sharon had been renting.

"You don't mind if I come along?" I asked, still feeling like an outsider despite Jay's determination to welcome me into his elite circle.

"You fit right in," he assured me. "You really never know who'll show up, day or night. Lots of interesting people."

The house sat hidden from view, tucked far back into the canyon up along a driveway protected by a gate. Despite the late hour, several lights were on as we approached.

"See, I told you there'd still be action here," said Jay, parking his Porsche alongside the other luxury cars. We walked past a little wishing well and went into the house.

Sharon greeted me warmly with a kiss on the cheek. "What can I get you to drink, Jim?" she asked.

"Hey, I'll have what Jay's having," I said, determined to follow his lead. She handed me a Heineken beer, which I'd never really liked much, but I didn't say anything.

She made some introductions. "This is my friend Abigail and her boyfriend Wojciech."

Everybody was lounging around in the softly-lit room. I felt like a deer in headlights. I nodded in greeting and said, "Nice to meet you all."

Sharon sat beside Jay on the couch; everybody resumed their conversations, laughing and passing around joints. Patting her belly, Sharon waved it away with a smile.

That night, I didn't pay much attention to the décor of the house. The women all looked beautiful, but very natural with no makeup.

The latest hits of the Mamas and Papas, The Doors, and The Rolling Stones were playing on a stereo in the background. Everybody was really relaxed and just having fun. The only one who wasn't relaxed was me. I just didn't say much.

Throughout the evening, though, I couldn't help but notice Sharon. Like Jay, she had a sort of star power. She reminded me of a cross between Nancy Sinatra and Twiggy, but prettier. She was earthy, hospitable, and a perfect blend of high fashion and hippie chic. If she and Jay were a couple, as I suspected, he was a lucky man.

Takeaways

- Leave the past in the past. What matters is the challenge right in front of you.

- Envision yourself succeeding.

- Keep honing the skills of the craft, even if it costs you money to learn.

- We'll keep repeating the same mistakes until we master the lesson and graduate to the next level.

- Sometimes the most unexpected relationships develop if you believe you belong in those circles too.

- Respect given is respect earned.

INGREDIENT #6

DON'T DANCE WITH GHOSTS

B usiness was booming in Albuquerque. My partner and friend Bill had invested all his time and energy into the shop, causing his marriage to bust up too. He'd recently met a woman named Rose, who'd become his new focus. Determined to make this relationship work, he wanted to decrease his work hours, get married to Rose and build her a house. I would buy out his shares.

My buddy Bob Papin, a client and used car dealer from Farmington, had wanted in on the Sebring action for a long time. "Listen, Jim," he said on one of his jaunts to Albuquerque. "I bought a plane. Why don't we go in on it together? And I'll throw in my car dealership as collateral."

That sounded good to me. I took him as a partner in my Sebring shop and in my four-state territory distributorships.

I welcomed sales calls and opening new accounts. Papin, who was a real good checker player and one of the few people who could give me a run for my money, would handle the accounting, books, and business activities.

We'd fly into town. I'd do my demos or training classes, and then we'd go out on the town after I'd finished. Balding and left with a limp from his military days, Papin was a real character—a funny guy who appointed himself my wingman.

With the boom in clientele, I now faced two big challenges. The first was hiring and training enough stylists to serve our growing list of clients. The second was managing all my accounts who were selling Sebring products in their shops.

I already had a lot on my plate, but I'd become addicted to landing new accounts. And I was good at it. I kept building the business in the way that I had proven successful—by choosing a new town, finding the best barbers in that particular community, and delivering cold-calls until I'd registered about 10 barbers to come to a demonstration of the Sebring method. If they agreed to buy the $380 worth of product, then I'd educate them in a two-day class on the Sebring cutting and styling technique. Of course, I'd also emphasize our daily shampooing, conditioning, and blow-drying recommendations.

Once again, I wanted to be the best—always. I improved upon the Roffler training course I'd taken at the start of my career and gave our Sebring students more bang for their buck, establishing the most extensive professional education program for stylists of that time.

These efforts paid off, as the classes yielded not only the initial fee, but also profitable repeat orders for the Sebring products. It didn't take long for our footprint to grow substantially, with many participants receiving official certification as Sebring stylists, many of which would open Sebring shops of their own.

Over the more than two years I'd been working with Jay, I'd flown all over the state and opened about 75 certified shops as accounts selling Sebring product in New Mexico. I also certified about 250+ individual barbers. Things had really begun to take off in Texas, too.

I stopped in Lubbock on a whim and wound up hitting the jackpot. I got even better results in Dallas when the top barber in town signed on with me. In the Lone Star state, we had about 100 certified Sebring shops with 300 plus barbers certified in the Sebring technique.

It was such a big area to cover, and even with a private plane at my disposal, I didn't have much time to spare building up the Sebring name in Colorado and Arizona. But everywhere I went, I was having tremendous success. Now Jay Sebring became even more than a mentor. He'd become my friend.

Together, we cooked up another event—a party advertising his appearance at my shop. He flew into town the third week in July 1969 for the festivities.

After the party, which attracted more than 100 guests, we traded haircuts like we usually did whenever we saw each other. I knew exactly how he liked to wear it. "Jim, you're the only one I trust to get it right," he said, as he sat in my chair looking in the mirror. "What do you say we hit that club where you took me last time I was in town?"

Once again, Jay's arrival generated a media frenzy. The next day, a local newspaper photographer snapped a few shots of Jay and me together in my shop. That photo ran in the July 24, 1969, edition of the local newspaper.

I was in my Sebring International Shop in Albuquerque around 10 in the morning on Saturday cutting one of my regulars when the top-of-the-hour news crackled over the radio: *Five people were found gruesomely murdered at a house in Benedict Canyon near Beverly Hills, California, this morning, including the actress Sharon Tate.*

The date was August 9, 1969, less than a month since I'd flown to California and partied with Jay, Sharon, and their friends at her house. I became very concerned.

An hour later, I received a call from John Madden, vice president of Sebring. He cut right to the chase: "Jim, I've got terrible news. Jay and Sharon were found murdered this morning at her house. The police don't have any suspects."

I was confused as I tried to process the information. "I don't understand, John. What does this mean?"

"All I know is that the police are calling it the most horrific crime scene they've ever encountered. From the looks of it, Jay put up a helluva fight. I'm guessing he was trying to protect Sharon." He grew quieter. "You know, she was pregnant and all."

After a long pause, he cleared his throat and continued. "Listen, Jim, I know this is a shock. Hell, we're all feeling it, but I have to ask you... Would you be willing to come out to LA and take over for Jay? We've got all his clients lined up for appointments, and. . . you're the only one I know he would have trusted with this."

My friend and creative mentor, who had decided to take a chance on me, was now gone forever. John was right about one thing. I *was* in shock. My brain was spinning and I had trouble absorbing John's request. What he was asking slowly sank in, and Jay's eerily prophetic statement came back to me: "If anything were to ever happen to me, I'd want you to take over for me, Jim," his voice echoed in my head.

There was only one answer. "Of course," I said.

Over the past two years, Jay had entrusted me with his secrets and brought me into his inner circle. We'd talked endlessly about the business, and I was determined to carry on his legacy. I wanted to ensure that his name would be remembered for all he had accomplished in his life.

I didn't think about how unlikely a successor I was or worry about giving up the nice living I'd established for myself in Albuquerque. I just knew I could not and would not fail my friend.

Jay's funeral took place four days after the murders and was attended by every leading man in Hollywood. Steve McQueen delivered the eulogy. And while I wanted to be there for the services, I was hurrying to wrap things up in New Mexico so I could relocate to Los Angeles. This meant contacting as many as 200 of my clients.

The brutality of the slayings was particularly horrific, and the details had left me wrecked with grief. A rope had been tied around both Jay and Sharon's necks, and they'd been stabbed numerous times. In addition, Jay had been shot. Three additional bodies had been discovered across the property, each holding multiple injuries. Coffee heiress Abigail Folger and her boyfriend Wojciech Frykowski. These were the people I'd met at the house when I had visited. The crime scene details terrorized the nation, and questions loomed over the case.

From the moment I'd first heard the radio report, I'd returned to survival mode. For me, that no longer meant running away like I had done so many times as a kid. I'd learned by now to handle the hard blows by standing my ground and fighting with all I had in me. But I'd learned something else by now, too—I could not waste energy throwing wild punches and fighting enemies too big to beat.

As I tried to decide next steps, I thought about all those hours playing checkers against my friend in the barber shop. That wise, patient mentor had taught me the importance of developing strategy. Through studying my opponent and mapping out my next nine moves in advance, I'd improved as a player and could win almost every match.

In light of the murders, stepping into Jay's shoes in California seemed almost impossible, but I knew I couldn't react emotionally, or I'd blow it for sure. Every move I made in the next several months would have to be carefully weighed and calculated—just as in a checkers game or boxing match. I'd have to plan ahead if I stood any chance of sustaining his business.

I could have easily let fear of the unknown stop me. My friend had been murdered, and at that point no one knew why he'd been targeted, who had committed the crimes, or what they might do next. Jay had lived a glamorous life with a smooth sense of cool, and I had my concerns. I wasn't certain I could attain his statute. He left me big shoes to fill—very big shoes.

Aside from that, I'd also never lived anywhere but New Mexico for any real length of time. I was 25 years old and basically unknown in Hollywood. I'd have to prove myself every step of the way.

When John called back to tell me I'd not only be stepping into the shop to serve clients, but would also be named president of Sebring International, the pressure intensified. I'd have to quickly gain the confidence of the Sebring staff and Jay's celebrity clientele, while also getting my hands around the product business. The only way to deal with the surge of anxiety and emotion was to keep moving, never stop. I hadn't figured out any answers yet, but I did know one thing for sure: My future was in Hollywood. What I'd make of it would be up to me.

Time was ticking. I was scrambling to move to California as quickly as possible. While I was still wrapping things up in New Mexico, Jay's old assistant reached out to me.

"Paul Newman is on the books and I'm not sure what to do. He's at his home in New York City right now, and Jay always went to him."

I wanted to do exactly what Jay would have done, so I reserved a flight out of Albuquerque right away. Then I called to let Mr. Newman know I'd be in his neck of the woods, just in case he needed a haircut.

"You aren't making a trip especially for me, are you, Markham?"

"Oh, no," I insisted. "I've got business in the city and I figured you might be needing a trim."

"Okay, then come on by my apartment when you get into town," he said. "It's on 52nd and Fifth Avenue."

My goal was to keep Paul as a client, and this was my chance to prove I could do the job. The doorman sent me up to the penthouse. When I arrived, Paul answered the door. "Joanne's not here right now," he said. "Can I get you something, Markham? Something to drink?"

"I'm fine, Paul."

The apartment was decorated in a sophisticated way, but was still warm and inviting. The view was sensational. Paul took me back to the master bedroom, where I washed and conditioned his hair. I told him I wanted to cut it the way it grew to the left.

"Nope," he said. "Jay always told me the same thing, but I don't want it to go over there. I've had it this way my entire life, and that's how I want it."

I wasn't about to fight with him about that. If Jay couldn't win that battle, I certainly wasn't going to. It's strange, with Jay gone, I was continuing to learn lessons from him. Ultimately, you've got to respect the client's wishes.

After I finished cutting his hair, Paul looked in the mirror and said, "That's perfect." The review was all I could ask for from such an important client.

After that, I hurried back to Los Angeles and was staying with Sebring Product President John Madden and his family. Together, we'd commute to Los Angeles. John was determined to get me as prepared as possible to take on this role running the company.

From the moment I'd first met Jay Sebring more than two years earlier, I'd admired everything about the celebrity stylist. Not just for his technique, but also for the way he dressed, spoke, and conducted himself with clients. I'd been in awe of his way with women and admired his ability to handle the media.

By now, I'd matured enough to recognize my weaknesses, but I'd also beaten the odds enough that I hoped I could honor Jay's legacy and continue to grow the business he'd worked so hard to create.

There was only one major roadblock that neither John nor I knew how to tackle. As he ushered me into Jay's old office, announcing it would now be mine, he added a warning: "Don't use the phones. The FBI has our lines bugged." It turned out, one of the stylists was a suspect.

I eyed the phones nervously. "This is crazy, man."

He looked at me cautiously. "Yeah, they'll probably want to interview you at some point, too."

"Why? They know I was in Albuquerque when that all went down."

"Yes, but you'd been at the house with Jay and Sharon just a few weeks earlier. You might have seen something that you don't even realize could be important."

"I hadn't thought about that."

In addition to the ongoing investigation, the pressure of keeping the business rolling weighed heavily on my shoulders. As the new face of Sebring, I was not only serving Jay's clients, I was also in charge of the products, setting up distributors, making appearances, dealing with the press, and more—lots more. I was caught in the middle of a whirlwind with hardly any time to process my emotions about anything.

Establishing credibility with Jay's exclusive clientele was critical to maintaining the company's high profile, so that was one of my top priorities. Almost immediately after my arrival that September, I started sending personal letters to Jay's large list of clients. In the letter, I introduced myself as his replacement and offered them each a free haircut. I also extended the offer to other celebrities beyond the established client list.

Peter Lawford was the first to take me up on the offer. Steve McQueen, Lee Marvin, and James Garner weren't far behind, along with a whole host of TV and film directors, writers, producers, and music industry heavyweights. I was surprised at how many others booked with me soon after the letter went out.

In addition to those bookings, my gamble on flying to New York City to cut Paul Newman's hair was paying off in spades.

I'd go to his home on Maple Street in Beverly Hills. I'd never seen such an enormous house. I guess it was about 8,000 square feet. His wife, actress Joanne Woodward answered the door with a sweet smile. She was even more beautiful in person, and I detected a slight southern drawl. She ushered me into Paul's movie room where he was watching the cuts from one of his not-yet-released films.

Paul grinned and stood as we entered. "Good to see you again, Markham. A lot shorter commute for you this time, huh?" Little did I know, that would prove to be the beginning of a longstanding friendship.

Determined to start integrating into my new city, I moved into the Farmer's Daughter Motel on Fairfax. It was cheap and it sat within walking distance of the shop, but it was a depressing place, with prostitutes and drug addicts on the corner. Certainly not the life I'd moved to California for, but it was a start.

The mood at the shop was understandably tense. The police still had no solid leads on the murders, and everyone was a suspect. No one really knew if Jay was a target or simply in the wrong place at the wrong time. I quickly got the vibe that I was viewed by many of the stylists as an outsider. They considered me an interloper on their turf—at worst, a gold digger. Many of them had been working for Jay for many years. I couldn't blame them for resenting me as I began to take over the company.

At times, I'd overhear the stylists refer to me as "Mr. Albuquerque."

I knew I'd proven myself to Jay, but the staff knew nothing of my hard-won business experience. They didn't know I was an award-winning stylist who'd been successful as Jay's first franchisee. And they didn't know I'd set up educational programs for Sebring across four states. I'd been training other stylists and opening accounts across my territories all while working as a Sebring distributor. I knew how to sell product, and that's where we were staking the future of Sebring International. I had a lot to teach my new staff, but first I'd have to earn their trust.

Dear Mr. Markham,

As I remember, and read again, the eulogy of
Jay Sebring given by Alvin Greenwald on August 13,
the trait of my son's character shone forth as we
all knew him. The accolade given in the venture
of his enterprise was not for him alone....but is
also attributable to you. In this we are very
proud. One man was the originator, the artist,
the spark and driving force; but Thomas (Jay)
alone did not fulfill the job.

I say to you that it also was your loyalty and
perseverance that made a large contribution.
Thence for your benefit and his remembrance, I
am sure you will continue with great fortitude.

So I close with strong feeling from Margarette, his
mother, and I, joined by Fred, his brother, Gerry
and Peggy, his sisters -- to express our heartfelt
appreciation to you for the expression of sympathy
in the hour of sorrow.

Sincerely,

Bernard J. Kummer
Detroit, Michigan
August 28, 1969

Letter to Jim from Jay Sebring's father
Bernard Kummer

Jay's parents, Mr. and Mrs. Kummer, came to Los Angeles to settle his estate about a month after his funeral. His mother was sweet and warm, while his father was a stern, no-nonsense accountant. After seeing how hard I was working to honor Jay's legacy, Mr. Kummer offered to let me move into his house. "No sense in you paying rent when Jay's place is sitting there empty," he said, assuring me they both fully supported me as their son's successor.

While they were in town, the police released Jay's Porsche from the crime scene on Cielo Drive. As the estate's executor, Mr. Kummer offered to sell the car to me. Jay and I had spent several cool evenings speeding around town in that car, so it came with sentimental value and memories that were priceless. I agreed to buy the car for $4,700.

The only catch was that I would need to go to the house where the murders took place and pick it up. The car had been sitting there all this time as part of an active crime scene.

When John dropped me off to pick up the car, I was overcome by emotions. I sat in the driver's seat for a few moments. I couldn't help but think of the horror that had happened on this property. My hands were shaking and my mind began to spin. It wasn't just grief that hit me. I was thinking, *What if this car is wired for a bomb?* I knew the idea was absurd since the police had likely been over everything, but my thoughts were racing and I was beginning to feel a little paranoid. Finally, I steadied myself and turned the ignition. It started right up, engine purring.

I breathed a sigh of relief.

Once back at the shop, I parked exactly where Jay had always parked. Amos Russell met me at the car. He'd long worked as a valet at the shop and was always willing to shine a customer's shoes, wash their cars, or bring them coffee or tea. He was a client favorite, sometimes drawing higher tips than the stylists, and he'd been working under Jay for quite a while.

"Let me have the key, Mr. Markham," he said gently in his southern accent, still strong despite his many years in Los Angeles. "I'll get her looking brand-new for you."

As I handed Amos the keys, he wiped away a tear.

One thing was for sure, Jay had been loved by many.

When I finished at the office for the week, I moved into Jay's house with a few of my belongings. The house remained just as Jay had left it—tastefully decorated and immaculate. The location was perfect, too. It was about six miles from the salon at the top of a road just off Benedict Canyon.

I should have been relieved to escape the hotel room on the rough corner of town, but I'd always struggled with insomnia and that night proved particularly tough. After hours of tossing and turning, I finally fell into a fitful sleep with the TV on for white noise.

At 4:00 a.m. loud noises jolted me awake. My heart was in my throat as another loud series of bangs rang out. It sounded as if someone was running across the roof. I leaped out of bed and ran to the kitchen, grabbing the longest, sharpest knife I could find. Shaking, I peered outside into the dark, but I couldn't see anything. Heavy clouds shrouded the moon as I waited, hearing nothing more than my heavy breathing.

The same thing happened the next night—and the next. I was completely unnerved, jumping at every noise and creak. Finally, I realized racoons had been gaining access to the roof from the hill behind the house. That knowledge offered little comfort in the wee hours when I would lie in the dark and imagine Jay's murderers coming to take me out.

After a week of living in fear, I could stand it no more. I returned the keys to Mr. Kummer and moved into an apartment in Brentwood. It was time for me to let Jay go and focus on saving his company.

Takeaways

- If the next step doesn't intimidate you, you aren't dreaming big enough.

- Block out the critics and haters.

- Train your mind to believe you deserve success, and then act the part.

- Prepare for the biggest role you can imagine.

- Recognize your weaknesses and work hard to improve.

- Guard your energy. You cannot run on an empty tank.

INGREDIENT #7

KEEP YOUR EMOTIONS IN CHECK

O nce I took over at the salon, I became close with Sharon Tate's family. Her father, Colonel Tate, was working closely with the FBI, hoping to solve the case. Sharon's mother, Doris Tate, occasionally invited me to join their family meals on the weekends—insisting from the start, like all her friends, I call her by her middle name, Gwen.

She treated me like I imagined a mother would. I'd never encountered a woman with such strong maternal instinct, and I admit I enjoyed the kindness. For her part, I think staying connected to me helped her feel connected to her daughter. She'd always loved Jay and treated him like a son, and in many ways, I was her last link to the two.

Gwen seemed to take comfort in sharing stories about Jay and Sharon, and it helped me deal with my grief as well. One night after dinner, she was talking about how much Sharon was looking forward to becoming a mother. "Jay was excited, too," she said. "You know, I wouldn't say this to anyone, but Jim, I think the baby was his."

I didn't say anything in response, but her statement was in line with what I'd witnessed. Sharon and Jay had behaved more like an intimate couple than platonic friends—something Vidal Sassoon would later relay to me from his encounter with the couple. Gwen's assumption seemed on point to me, and while nothing was ever officially announced, I've always assumed that the unborn child was Jay's.

In early December 1969, John Madden and Jay's parents—Mr. and Mrs. Kummer—booked a press conference and party at The Factory, an exclusive club in Hollywood. They authorized a press release officially announcing me as Jay's successor and formally introducing me as president of Sebring International. Celebrities like Peter Lawford attended and the press was out in force that evening. The wave of publicity was my first experience of that magnitude. My new role as the face of Sebring made the news on all the TV stations, major newspapers, magazines, and radio.

A week later, the police made arrests in the murders of Jay Sebring, Sharon Tate, and the other victims at Cielo Drive. Self-proclaimed cult leader Charles Manson had ordered his followers (known as "the Family") to commit these murders. The official police theory was that Manson had chosen that house because that belonged to record producer Terry Melcher, the son of actress Doris Day. Melcher had expressed interest in Manson's music, but eventually turned him down. Charlie Manson had become obsessed with the Beatles' *White Album* and in particular the song *Helter Skelter*. Investigators suspected he'd ordered the brutal murders as part of a warped plan to start a race war.

I wasn't the only one in Jay's circle who wasn't fully on board with that theory.

In a salon, you hear a lot of gossip. People sit in your chair and sometimes use it like a confessional. Rumors had been swirling around that Charlie had focused on that house because it was known to attract some of Hollywood's A-list celebrities. It seemed common knowledge that Manson desperately wanted to be famous.

In my circle, many thought that sometime before the murders, Charlie had come to the gate and offered to sell drugs to Jay and

Wojciech. Instead of making a deal, Manson had become violent and an altercation took place among Jay, Wojciech, and Charlie. Some speculated that Manson had sent the Family up there in retaliation.

There were three or four other scenarios floating around. When I got the news of the arrests, I felt relief. The FBI investigation was finally behind us. Still, I couldn't shake a feeling of unease that had tormented me since I was a boy. I called my mom as soon as I heard the news. I told her about the reports and said I was calling to check on her.

"Oh, I'm fine, Jimbo," she said. "You know me. Nothing keeps me down for long."

A car horn sounded on the other end of the line. "Listen, son, I gotta go. A friend's picking me up."

Before I could say goodbye, she'd already hung up. Her fifth husband had just divorced her, and I figured that *friend* was her new love interest. I knew what they had in common was the bottle.

Once again, I was left worrying that either her addiction to men or to alcohol would be the death of her. I carefully placed the receiver in its cradle with a sigh. I'd never been able to protect her when I was living with her. Why should anything be different now?

From the time of the Manson family's arrest in mid-December 1969 and throughout 1970, my relationship with the Tate family grew against the agonizing backdrop of the murder trial that they attended faithfully. We never talked about the murders, despite all the gruesome details being laid bare in the courtroom and being churned out by the press daily.

Despite the emotional strain, I'd continued moving forward, believing I could best serve Jay by saving his company. I soon realized Sebring International had a lot of problems lurking under the surface. Like so many things in Tinseltown, appearances can be deceiving.

While adjusting to my new position at Sebring, I'd spent little time socializing with the celebrities outside of work. Not only had I been struggling to save the business, I had to navigate the emotional turbulence of the murder investigation and subsequent trial. I was afraid of saying the wrong thing or coming off like a small-town boy.

I kept my mouth shut and usually found reasons not to accept the social invitations that came my way. But John Madden had been pressuring me to take over Jay's membership at The Candy Store in order to "keep up the image." It was the place to be seen, he argued, and everybody who was anybody in Hollywood hung out there.

One night I was settled into a table with a couple of beautiful women, when a man walked up and said, "This is Mr. Sinatra's table. You gotta move."

I nodded, but felt defiant. I didn't like being told I *had* to do anything. I went right back to talking, my mind focused solely on the women. A few minutes later, two men approached our table and said, "Mr. Sinatra's here. You have to leave. Now."

I guess I didn't move fast enough for them, because the two men exchanged a glance and then got on either side of me, each grabbing an arm and lifting me up off the ground. They carried me all the way to the other side of the room and set me back down in a way that meant business.

My face flushed. For the first time in a long time, that blind rage boiled from the pit of my stomach, up my chest and into my brain. I was embarrassed, humiliated. Everything in me wanted to fight.

Let it go, Jim.

I went to the men's room to cool down. After a few deep breaths, I took a hard look at myself in the mirror.

You do belong, Markham, I told myself. *You are here among the A-listers for a reason. Go back out there and enjoy the evening.*

Thankfully, I was able to get my emotions under my control and not be triggered to react as I'd done so many times in the past. Because I was finally able to respond as the new Jim, and not as the young traumatized boy I'd been trying to protect during all those years of fighting, Frank Sinatra got his table for the night and became my loyal customer within the year.

By the end of January 1970, John Madden, 6'2" and a fast-talker with a booming voice, added another must-do to my overwhelming list. He announced that he'd arranged for me to provide a product demonstration at Buffums, a department store in San Diego.

Jay had been doing in-store appearances in upscale department stores across Southern California, but I'd never seen him in action. I protested, trying to explain my shortcomings to John as well as my concerns about the finances. "Besides," I added, "I don't think that's the route we should be going."

"We've already got the ads running for it," he insisted, giving me a big toothy grin. "I'll go with you. It'll be fine."

I was unconvinced.

We headed to Buffums. A large sign announced my appearance, and our products were displayed on a nearby counter. I'd brought a model along with me, but anxiety set in as I worried about demonstrating a cut and style effectively while at the same time entertaining shoppers enough to sell product—our ultimate goal.

Just as I was getting ready to start, John disappeared.

I was scared to death, because I had everything to lose. With no Plan B, I realized if I couldn't pull the company back to financial sustainability, there could be trouble.

With John nowhere in sight, I fulfilled my obligation, speaking to half a dozen women who stopped for a few minutes to watch.

Only two men were in the audience. I don't think we sold a single thing.

That flop confirmed my thinking that our current approach was wrong.

I pointed out my concerns to John: Women weren't our target audience. Men were unlikely to come into a department store, much less to hang around a demonstration. The stores were slow to pay. Some were claiming that the product was separating in the bottle. There were also problems with the hairspray.

John didn't know how to address these issues I was facing. Our cash flow wasn't just tight—it was non-existent. We both understood we had to get money in the door. And fast.

The only way I knew to do this was to open accounts like I'd done as Jay's distributor. During the time I was working with Jay, I'd gotten 640 barbers certified in the Sebring method. Each account had received two days of training in exchange for purchasing about $400 worth of product. The barbers became retailers and bought the products like crazy and sold them to their customers. Barbers had never done retailing before. It was a brand-new market.

Unlike the department store buyers, the barbers loved Sebring products, because they were the best on the market. If the conditioner separated in the bottle, they just shook it up. The department store business just kept declining. It was killing us.

Now I needed to clone myself. Our only hope was to create distributors who could open accounts and lead the education as I'd done in my four-state territory. Only one other men's hair care company was using this strategy of selling exclusively to barbers and training them to be experts. We had plenty of room to grow. We just needed more feet on the ground.

With this in mind, I addressed the issue of the product separation and met with our chemist at BG Labs. He was a man named Goody. He was tall, in his early 60s, and wore a gray hairpiece. He had a small warehouse where he and his sons would mix our shampoo in 55-gallon drums and then mix it with a propeller. Before he started making Sebring shampoo and conditioner, his main product was dog shampoo.

When I told him about the problem we were having with the conditioner separating, he simply shrugged his shoulders and said, "I'll do my best to figure this out, Jim." It wasn't a very scientific approach. He'd give me the new batch to try out on my customers, and I'd set it in the sun in my office to see if it separated.

He never was able to figure out how to adjust the formula to get the last 1/2 teaspoon of the hairspray out of the can. He kept trying, but finally told me, "That's just the way it is."

Together, we worked to find the perfect scent, something that seemed a better fit for our distinctive red logo and sleek black bottles. To achieve the level of success that Sebring deserved, our products needed to be excellent—not just good enough. We already had a hard sell by trying to convince men to wash and condition daily. We couldn't afford to sell products that were anything less than the best out there. Despite my inexperience and his somewhat makeshift operation, we managed to create magic.

Because getting cash in the door was so critical, I decided we should sell exclusively through professional salons and barber shops and ditch department stores altogether. The first thing I had to do was convince barbers that the Sebring method was superior, or else they'd never buy our products. I went back to my tried-and-true method. With each cold call, I introduced myself, explaining that my clients were Hollywood's elite and that I charged $50 a haircut. That was at least 10 times the amount most barbers were getting at the time, and that got the conversation started.

Next, I asked if I could come and do a demo, requesting that they invite other barbers in town to attend, too. They had to believe that I had something to teach them or it was game over. I not only showed the barbers a better way to cut hair, I taught them that they could charge higher prices for haircuts by becoming a men's hair styling expert. I also showed them that they could make additional money by retailing Sebring products. Hardly any barbers were selling hair care items at the time.

If a barber decided to become a distributor, carving out a small territory of his own, he'd pay $5,000 for that right. I'd train them as certified Sebring stylists.

Their shops would also become Sebring certified, which meant I'd explain how to use and sell our products as well as how to teach other barbers to become certified and open other accounts. The process was exhausting at times, especially because most of the guys at the top had been cutting and styling their own way for years. As with anything, the resistance to change proved intense.

To find the right distributors required that I be on the road nearly non-stop. I tried not to come back to the office until I'd sold three or four distributorships per month. I got the cash up front before I shipped them any product. That required that I become a creative salesman, quickly assessing each room and adjusting my presentation accordingly. I learned to develop patience and persistence.

I'll never forget the top barber in Ames, Iowa. Over a Saturday and into Sunday afternoon, he repeatedly told me, "Let me see you do just one more haircut, Jim. I want to be sure this is really the best technique."

By the time I finally got that $5,000 out of him, I'd probably cut a dozen of his customers for free! It was worth it, though. He became one of my best distributors.

After removing Sebring products from department stores, our sales shot up. Within 90 days of deploying my new strategy, I had us back in the black. But by the time I finally came off the road and returned to the office, a mutiny was underway.

One male stylist had managed to convince five others to join him at a shop he'd opened down the street. Another took four others with him to a new place, leaving just five on the floor to handle all of our clients. While such uprisings aren't uncommon for salons, this one couldn't have come at a worse time. Added to my already full plate, I now needed to find and train stylists who would be comfortable working with the elite level of clientele Sebring attracted.

I was already working 16-hour days to keep the shop afloat. I'd been devoting every ounce of energy into making Sebring profitable. On top of that, I was still servicing the territories for my own distributorship and keeping an eye on our franchised shops—one of which I still owned with my partner Bob Papin back in Albuquerque. But my primary focus was on two things: keeping our celebrity clients feeling special, and selling more distributorships, which was our key to financial growth.

Within the first year, I not only had maintained our A-list clients, I'd turned Sebring around from losing $20,000 a month to earning $20,000 a month in profits.

That spring, one of my Sebring accounts from Farmington moved to Denver to take on the Sebring distributorship. In May, he called me excited because he'd secured the rights to open a Sebring certified shop in the Playboy Club in Denver.

"Now, that's a first!" I said, congratulating him over the phone.

"Can you come to the grand opening, Jim? I'd love to have you here."

"Of course, I'll come." I joked that he didn't need to ask twice to get me to join him at the Playboy Club.

When I arrived in Denver, my publicist had lined up media appearances with TV, radio, magazines, and the local newspaper, the

Denver Post, which ran a feature story about me giving $52 haircuts to the world's top stars (I'd raised the price a couple bucks). It was a publicity bonanza. Radio, TV stations, and magazines were on hand to cover the grand opening. But the best part was that I hit it off with the *Denver Post* reporter and she agreed to join me for dinner.

There was only one hitch. I was supposed to be in Las Vegas to cut Jack Entratter's hair. Jack was one of the founding fathers of Las Vegas and owner of The Sands Hotel. Nicknamed "Mr. Entertainment," Jack was an elite client I'd inherited from Jay. Every 11 days I'd fly to Las Vegas, where he'd put me up in a suite. While there, I could go to any show I wanted, and all my food was comped. I could go anywhere in town and say, "Jack sent me." Those magic words always got me to the front of any line. I'd cut his hair along with anyone else he'd brought in, usually a few club owners and business associates. Each haircut brought me $100, but the trip was usually a wash because I loved playing blackjack a little too much.

During a break in the Denver hubbub, I called Jack and requested a one-day change in our schedule. "I'm in the middle of doing interviews for our new Sebring shop at the Playboy Club in Denver," I explained. "Could I come tomorrow instead?"

There was dead silence on the other end of the line. He replied with two words, "Come tonight."

A chill ran down my spine. I knew I had a problem, and it could become a big one going forward with the kind of schedule I was keeping. Jack, who was associated with mobster Meyer Lansky, was tight with Frank Sinatra. He'd built the Copa Room at The Sands especially for "The Chairman" and leader of the Rat Pack. Frank, whom I'd started cutting at my Sebring office, had recorded his live album at The Sands in 1966. When Jack came to Hollywood, he'd always summon me to the Beverly Hills Hotel to cut his hair.

I understood from those two words, "Come tonight," that my presence that evening was a command performance and assured him that I would be there as originally scheduled. Still considered the new kid in town, I could not afford to alienate any of my clients—especially Jack. I had to deliver, even if it meant losing the date with Denver's hottest journalist. I dared not cross him.

Takeaways

- Just because you're in a hole doesn't mean you can't find your way out of it.

- When one way isn't working, try another way.

- Don't give in to the IMPOSTER SYNDROME. You are good enough.

- Teach others what you know and let them help you meet your goals.

- Never let emotions overrule reason.

INGREDIENT #8

FROM THE MINORS
TO THE MAJORS

There are times in my life when answers don't come easily. I find myself standing at a podium surrounded by journalists and various TV news reporters. It's December 2nd, 1969, and I'm at The Factory night club in West Hollywood at 1:30 in the afternoon on an unseasonably hot day.

Actor Peter Lawford introduces me to the audience of more than 100 people. Today, I am officially named president of Sebring International. Ironically, after more than three months, the LAPD has taken into custody a group of young men and women believed to be responsible for Jay and Sharon's murder. Bernard Kummer, Jay's father and his mother, Margarette, stand beside me as photographers snap our picture.

There's a sense of relief throughout Los Angeles, and though there is much excitement about the future of Jay's company moving forward with me at the helm, there is also loneliness and uncertainty for me in my new city.

I find myself lost for words as I attempt to answer questions. "How do you think Jay would have felt about YOU as his replacement?" "What makes you qualified for this position?" "Where do you see the company a year from now?"

Peter Lawford gives me a smile and a wink as I politely tell journalist

Lydia Lane that Sebring International will continue to advance with our innovative product line, unique cutting method, and our clientele will still be served with the first-class treatment in men's hair care that Jay made famous.

Jay's lawyer, Alvin Greenwald, comes over and shakes my hand and says, "I believe Jay would be happy that you've been the one chosen to carry on his legacy." Respectfully, I thank him.

Today is the beginning of something big, and I have butterflies in the pit of my stomach. I take a moment to reflect: This is both the scariest and most exciting time in my life. I've been called up to replace the star and captain of this major company because of a tragedy.

No matter how you look at it, *I'm in the big leagues now.* And everything I do from this day on will be looked at under an intense magnifying glass. Jealousy from many of the Sebring stylists is just something I will have to learn to deal with.

Here, I stand alone. And like with any initial shock, I know when it wears off, I WILL deliver.

One of my other new relationships continued to grow stronger. For some reason, Paul Newman had taken special interest in me from the start. In the summer of 1970, he issued an invitation I couldn't turn down.

"Jim, we're getting ready to make *Sometimes a Great Notion.* We'll be filming in rural Oregon," he said. "It's about a family of loggers. I'd like you to come style the principal actors on the set."

"I'd be honored," I said, hardly believing my luck.

I flew up to Oregon, and he was there at the gate to meet me.

Paul Newman was undeniably handsome, with a great sense of humor and exceptional taste. On this film, Paul was not only the leading man, he was also directing for only his second time.

On the way to location, Paul couldn't resist showing me how fast his new Corvette could go. Sure enough, here came the blue flashing lights.

But Paul didn't play the celebrity card to get out of the situation. Instead, he was a class act—polite and respectful to the officer. When the cop noticed one of world's most famous actors sat behind the wheel, he shook his head and told him, "Slow it down, sir." And then he sent us on our way without a ticket.

That situation was just one of many in which I observed Paul's good nature. Despite being one of the most esteemed sex symbols of the era, he managed to be down to earth.

When I went with him on location, a new challenge arose. On set, I had to pay attention to the finest details for continuity's sake. A film might be shot over the course of several months. But in each scene, the star needed to look the same—as if he hadn't had a haircut and didn't need one either. Once I was on set, I realized what a big challenge this presented. That meant I not only had to style and cut Paul's hair, but also the hair of Henry Fonda, Michael Sarrazin, Richard Jaeckel, and the actress Lee Remick.

The second challenge was learning how to hurry up and wait. Although I was so impressed with watching the actors create scenes and do what they do, I quickly learned that a lot of my job involved standing around. Then, all of the sudden, I'd be called in and had 35 minutes or so to cut their hair in between scenes. Sometimes I was cutting hair while Paul sat on a log or outside his trailer. I never knew where I'd be working.

On the movie, the crew became close. It started to feel like family to me. It was fun being on location.

Paul talked to me about what it took to be an actor. He'd joke around on the set, but when the cameras were rolling, he was serious and focused.

I would fly up about every 12 days. Scenes were often shot out of sequence, so I had to make sure their hair looked exactly the same throughout the filming of the movie.

When the time came for the wrap party, I was invited. Shirley MacLaine, Richard Jaeckel, John Forman, and the director George Roy Hill all made an effort to include me, but I still felt so out of place.

The only thing that helped me in that moment was when I remembered what Paul had told me during one of our many talks: "A seasoned actor I admired told me a long time ago, 'Stop acting the part and become the character.' Once I did that, I became a much better actor."

Over the next several years, I too began to use that philosophy.

The experience of being on a movie set gave me an opportunity to practice my method—honing my craft to a new level as I worked to build that quality of consistency into every style.

My final day on the set, Paul called me to his trailer. "Markham, I know this was your first time on a movie, but I've got to tell you something—you fit right in, and you're good at this. So good, in fact, that I'm going to make sure you get a credit."

I was floored. That possibility hadn't even occurred to me. A barber had never been given a movie credit before. "Thank you, Paul," I said. "You have no idea what this means to me."

After my time on location in Oregon, I returned to Los Angeles. John Madden, who'd taken the title of president of Sebring Products, called me into his office. "We need to talk about your future here," he said, smiling. "I want to offer you 1 percent of Sebring."

I was astonished. I'd been given the title of president of Sebring International, but that income only encompassed the salon and a modest take-home salary. The reality was, I was doing my job and his, too. I knew John had taken Jay's 67 percent and that what he was proposing wasn't anywhere close to a reasonable offer—especially after all that I'd done to save the company from financial ruin.

"I was thinking more like 10 percent," I said.

His eyebrows shot up. "Really? Well, that's not going to happen. So where does that leave us?"

I was used to being underestimated. I'd learned to size up my opponents from my days of boxing and racing motorcycles. Dropping out of school in the ninth grade, I became street smart. Competing in so many hair cutting and styling competitions, had taught me how important it is to prepare and pay attention to the minor details.

Once again, I was sitting across from someone who'd underestimated me. John mistook my youth for naiveté, forgetting even though I was in my mid-20s, that I'd already been in the industry almost a decade.

"That's not going to happen," I said to him.

"Well, take it or leave it."

"I'm not taking that," I said.

"Well, then I don't know what to tell you."

I was steamed and I walked out. I plotted my next move, realizing my every step from that point on would have to be carefully taken.

My first year at the helm of Sebring International flew by. I was on the road constantly, working to expand our product sales. Finally, on January 25, 1971, after a six-month trial, Charles Manson and his followers were convicted on all 27 counts of murder and sentenced to the death penalty.

Shortly after, my ex-wife Lena called, catching me during one of my rare moments of sitting at my desk in my office. "Jim, we need to talk," she said with a serious tone. "It's about our son, Jay."

My heart raced at the thought of anything being wrong with him. "Is he okay?" The last time, I'd gone by to see him, she held him in her arms the entire time; he cried when I tried to take him from her.

"He's fine," she said, her voice cold and flat. "But as you know, I'm remarried now, and my husband thinks it's a good idea for him to adopt Jay. He needs a proper family."

"Adopt? Why? He's my son, Lena. You know I visit every chance I get. I send money. I'm doing all I can for him."

"I think it's best, Jim, that he has just one father. It's too confusing otherwise."

My ears began to ring as I paced the office. "I don't understand. What are you saying?"

"I'm saying I don't want you to have any more contact with him until he turns 16. Then he'll be old enough to make his own decisions."

"Sixteen? Is this some kind of joke?" It was all I could do not to throw the phone across the room.

"No. I'm serious, Jim. Let Jay have this man as his father, and please don't stop by anymore when you're in the area. It'll just hurt him."

Before I could respond, she hung up.

I stood there—stunned. Everyone I'd ever loved had left me, but I couldn't believe my ex-wife was trying to erase me from my son's life.

With everything in a tangled mess, I did what I'd always done. I focused on the part of my life where I was winning. I stayed on track throughout the first year, still managing to meet my goal of signing two to four distributors per month.

In late May 1971, Jay Sebring's father, Bernard, who was an accountant, announced that he was putting the business into bankruptcy.

I was shocked and disappointed, because we'd steadily gained momentum over the past year and were in the middle of a viable turnaround when he, unfortunately, pulled the plug.

One night over a couple beers, Paul Newman asked me directly about Sebring International. "Markham, I've got $30,000 invested in the company," he said. "With this bankruptcy, I'm not sure what I ought to do. John's asked for my support."

I held nothing back. "Look, Paul, as far as I can tell, John is a pretty good salesman, but he was betting on the strategy of selling through department stores. I've been in this industry a long time, and I'm making these distributorships work, turning profits after years of operating in the red. I'm going to shoot straight with you here. I don't think John's the right one to lead Sebring into the future."

He nodded. "So you'd pull out?"

I looked him straight in the eye and said, "Yep. I think you should take it out."

He listened to me and withdrew his support. That was that. If Paul had not taken me at my word, John would have prevailed, and I likely would have gone back to Albuquerque.

Shortly after Sebring International and Sebring Products went into bankruptcy, Bernard put the assets of the companies up for auction. John Madden assumed he'd be the highest bidder. He had no idea that I'd scrambled and teamed up with two partners to bid on the name, the shop, and the product line. Bob Papin, my friend from back in Farmington, who had partnered with me to buy our plane, had wanted to be in business with me for a long time. With Sebring on the auction block, he jumped at the chance. Joanie Wyatt—who had been a publicist for Sebring and became a friend—also invested as a partner, assuring me she believed in my approach with the company and wanted to support those efforts.

We each pledged a third of our bid of $50,000, which easily beat out John Madden.

Although I loved the nonstop action of the Hollywood scene, I was shrewd enough to feel the clock ticking. We had to make Sebring an undeniable success—and fast.

My travel schedule, which took me across the United States, had proven brutal. But the only sure route I saw was to continue to convert the nation's most influential barbers to the Sebring method and then, if qualified, designate them as Sebring distributors for their territories.

Somehow, I kept up with all my celebrity clients while shifting into hyperdrive to find good distributors. The task was especially challenging because barbers rarely have the bandwidth to think beyond their one shop. Finding candidates who saw the opportunity and who could be trusted to head a small territory was a tall order. Sometimes I'd even accompany them to the bank, walking them through the entire loan process so they could pay the $5,000 necessary to keep the company afloat.

In my new role as president over both Sebring International and Sebring Products, I used my status as a celebrity stylist to generate plenty of publicity for distributors. My publicist, who was now my partner, had a vested interest in making that happen, so she kicked it up a notch, too.

I periodically called Papin from the road to find out how he was coming along with selling the Albuquerque shop and the Sebring distributor rights in New Mexico. I wanted those funds as a cushion. Since both pieces of business were thriving, I felt confident that finding a buyer would be a cinch.

Going into 90 days from the time we'd won the bid, our three-way partnership grew contentious, but all I knew to do was to keep forging ahead.

I had opened 35 distributors from the point that I'd taken over Sebring. I'd built the business up to more than 1,000 certified Sebring shops, and more than 3,000 barbers had earned their Sebring certification. Eventually, my two partners filed a lawsuit to try and kick me out of the company. When we couldn't settle the lawsuit, the court-appointed receiver declared that none of the three partners could work at Sebring until we reached an agreement.

Just like that, I was shut out.

My dream turned into a nightmare—only I was fully awake and living it. As long as litigation continued, I could no longer use my office or even go to the shop. My salary ceased immediately, and my club memberships were voided.

To generate cash, I started teaching the Sebring method in Orange County, California. Cutting hair using the Sebring method and teaching it had been my whole life going on five years. My former partners complained to the receiver, who put a stop to that quickly. I was no longer allowed to use the Sebring name or teach the Sebring classes.

I was done.

With no income, I soon had to give up my apartment. Papin had sold the plane, and because my name wasn't on the title, he kept the proceeds. I managed to keep up with Paul Newman and Peter Lawford, but without a place to call my own, most of my clients found other stylists to cut their hair.

After leaving the life I'd built in Albuquerque to come to Los Angeles at John's request, I'd become a ghost.

Still, I refused to quit and go back to New Mexico. I stayed with different girlfriends, relying on old tricks to make enough cash along the way. Only this time, as I hustled pool and played checkers for money, I was going up against the cut-throat pimps who controlled Sunset Boulevard.

Most of my opponents had learned checkers in prison. I'd learned in a barber shop. Games could be tense, but I'd usually win enough to keep me going for the next day or two. I was operating in survival mode once again.

At first, they suspected I was an undercover cop, but I kept coming back to the table until they eventually tolerated me and even seemed amused.

One night, Big Cecil—who must have outweighed me by more than 100 pounds at least—became furious when I ran the pool table on him after beating him at the two previous games of 8 Ball. As I reached to grab the stack of bills, he slapped his hand on top of mine.

"Let's take it out back," Big Cecil said. "Whoever comes back inside picks up the money."

I'm not going to lose this fight. I'm a winner and that's my money.

"Deal," I said between clenched teeth.

I was shaking. Not from fear, but from pent-up fury. I was tired of people taking what was rightfully mine. Cecil's stable of girls snickered, as several of the other pimps followed us out back into the parking lot.

Big Cecil took the first swing and missed. I threw one that bloodied his nose.

We each threw a flurry of punches, mine connecting more often than not.

I kept my hands up, protecting my face while holding his gaze. He may have outsized me, but I was a man who had nothing to lose. We fought to the point of exhaustion. Finally, he put his hands down and nodded at me.

I slowly lowered my hands and nodded back.

Without a word, I walked back into the pool hall, picked up the money, grabbed the hand of one of his girls, and escorted her out of the pool hall. The victory was mine.

Takeaways

- Necessity can bring the determination to dig deep.

- Understand your value.

- Be confident in your strengths.

- Fight for what's right.

- Once you lose your fear of failure, you start to think like a winner.

INGREDIENT #9

DARE TO BE DIFFERENT

After 18 months of intense negotiations, we finally settled the lawsuit in 1972. My former partners took control of Sebring International and Sebring Products, but I got the rights to half of their salaries—$30,000 a year for life. More importantly, I successfully negotiated the right to start a competing company.

Thankfully, I'd already lined up a partner and investor for my next act: a competing company called Markham Products. My attorney had raised $50,000 in seed money, and I'd convinced a few celebrity clients to invest—just as they had with Jay. I was determined to take everything I'd learned during my few years at the helm of Sebring and apply that knowledge to the company that would bear my own name.

In return for $50,000 for Markham Products, I put up the 33 1/3 of Sebring stock that I'd been awarded during the settlement. That served as the collateral, but I also agreed to pay 10 percent interest plus a significant portion of Markham stock.

Still, I owned 57 percent of the new company, and now instead of building someone else's legacy, I was free to build my own.

Peter Lawford had agreed to serve as my spokesperson in exchange for company shares. He'd also hit the road with me to do personal appearances at important hair shows, as well as appearing in radio spots and print advertisements. Vidal Sassoon had deployed a similar strategy in the women's market, but we were the first to use a celebrity spokesperson in the men's arena.

By coincidence, I started Markham Products on my 29th birthday —December 22, 1972. By April '73, we had a line of products ready to go. We packaged a specialized grooming kit that included Markham shampoo, conditioner, hair spray, a shampoo brush, and a brush comb with long teeth. With that kit, a customer had everything needed to replicate the style he was given in the shop. We also sold blow dryers to the distributors, who in turn sold them to other shop owners.

Once I launched Markham, Danny Kopels, an ad agency owner, was the first to reach out to me. Danny and I had hit it off a year earlier. He was one of the few people who kept up with me while my career was on the ropes. His loyalty meant a lot to me. He also seemed a kindred spirit, being an only child from the Bronx whose mother had died when he was just 16. I recognized him as a self-starter with that admirable drive to win, so I brought him in to head up advertising and marketing for a salary plus stock. He agreed with one condition: He could still work with his existing freelance clients. Like me, he wanted the freedom to do his own thing and didn't want to link his destiny to a single star.

Danny's first task was to design our prototype packaging. Initially, we rented one tiny room in the suite of a law firm. Neither of us knew all that much about manufacturing and packaging, but we were full of confidence and brimming with ideas. It didn't take long for Danny to come up with a new logo. "Dig this," he said, showing me a circle with a man inside it.

I clapped him on his back and said, "Let's go with it."

But that's when we hit our first snag. When the label was applied to the curved surface of the bottle, our cool new logo appeared to be oval-shaped. Danny went back to the drawing board and redesigned the logo to address the optical illusion.

That process taught me that mistakes don't have to be fatal, as long as you move swiftly to correct them. What matters is surrounding yourself with people who are willing to put in the effort to make things right as soon as a problem pops up. With that kind of partner or team, even mistakes can be fun.

We were operating in startup mode, which meant we needed to get cash in the door as quickly as possible. That also meant we needed a plan. For me, desperation was a powerful motivator. I was determined to succeed. But I also knew how easy it is for a new company to fail.

I focused on several key issues, trying to lay the foundation for success. First, I figured out our overhead and cash flow requirements monthly, quarterly, and annually. With an accountant's help, we formulated sales projections and a profit & loss statement for the first year. We needed to sell at least $20,000 worth of product per month just to break even. We had no breathing room. We couldn't outstrip the cashflow or the business wouldn't survive.

I packed my shears and hit the road immediately—determined to concentrate my efforts on methods that had worked in the past.

Men's hairstyling was in its infancy. With several major competition wins under my belt and a reputation as stylist to A-list stars like Paul Newman, Steve McQueen, and Johnny Carson, I was able to get my foot in the door of the best shops in every town I visited. My proposition was simple: I guaranteed I could triple their money, and if I couldn't show them a totally new and better way of doing things, they were under no obligation to buy.

I was one of the early pioneers of men's hairstyling. The Markham Method was revolutionary. My approach allowed men to grow out their hair and sideburns and adopt a cut and style which complemented not just their head and face shape, but their lifestyle. I encouraged men to ditch the Brylcreem and Vitalis of yesteryear in favor of a regimen of daily shampooing, conditioning, and styling with Markham Cherry Almond Shampoo, Cherry Almond Condition, and Markham Hair Control.

At first, some men felt this approach was too feminine. However, they were easy to convince otherwise when I explained that not only would their hair look better, but the regimen would promote healthier hair, and they would keep their hair longer. Integral to this promise was daily use of the Markham Shampoo Brush. The brush stimulated the scalp, increased blood flow, cleaned the follicle of dead skin and oil, and allowed the hair to grow in an easy manner—reducing hair loss. (The shampoo brush was so popular, I would bring it back with great success in later years not just for men, but women.)

At this time, the majority of shops didn't retail products. I focused on recruiting those who would not only sell products, but would recruit other owners to become certified in my styling technique—just as I'd done with my last company. Once an account was established as a certified Markham Style Innovator Shop, they would raise their prices, use my products, and retail them to their customers.

Signing up shops and selling them $5,000 of product became my highest priority. My self-imposed rule was that I stayed out on the road as long as it took each month in order to hit my goal. I didn't always hit the target, but by the end of our first year, I had blown past the break-even mark and our numbers swelled to over 100 Markham Style Innovator shops.

The downside was that I was constantly on the road. It was exhausting and lonely, but I couldn't afford to have an off day. I knew the critical importance of securing that strong base. I went wherever I thought I could do some business. Texas was one of my first territories. I also had good luck in Oklahoma, Arkansas, Pennsylvania, Georgia, and Alabama that first year.

The work was hard, but the concept was simple. I had to sell, sell, sell, or I'd be out of business. I got used to hearing "no" a lot. I never could crack Arizona for some reason. I couldn't even get anyone to let me do a demonstration there. Each time I'd hear another rejection, I'd remember Dale Carnegie's words: "If you haven't heard 'no' at least eight times, you didn't try hard enough." I persevered, and after several attempts, I finally did it—signing up the best shop in Scottsdale.

As I signed up more and more shops, they started ordering product and selling to their accounts. The pressure gradually eased up, but still, I didn't stop. I wasn't yet satisfied. There were 50 states, and I set my sights on making my mark in all of them.

We spent our meager advertising budget in the professional trade magazines creating a campaign around *10 Reasons Why You Should Be Markham*. I created a detailed business manual that explained everything needed to be a successful Markham Style Innovator shop. I also put together a public relations book, enabling certified shops to capitalize on our ad campaigns to get local publicity for their business. This included radio spots, ad slicks featuring Peter Lawford, and photos of the many stars who had converted to being my clients with Markham. By providing these tools, I gave shop owners exactly what I wished I would have had at my fingertips when I'd become the first Sebring franchisee. Eventually, my Markham distributors outsold the Sebring distributors in their respective markets by about 50 percent.

With the growth of Markham Products, we knew the importance of advertising and marketing to maintain momentum. We also knew we couldn't afford a shotgun approach. The Markham brand needed a targeted, memorable message. Danny Kopels and I agreed that every advertising, marketing, and public relations dollar we spent should yield a minimum of $10 in sales.

Our PR firm was Mahoney & Wasserman, who handled rock stars like the Rolling Stones and The Who. They mentioned how fans were going crazy over tour T-shirts that were sold at the rock concerts. They were becoming collectibles, much to everyone's surprise.

"You're kind of the rock star of the hair industry," Danny said. "Why not do something that will really grab attention—something that would be fun to wear on a T-shirt?" *Maybe he was onto something.*

I was known as the world's most expensive men's hair stylist (now charging $55). Why not capitalize on that? Inspiration struck. We came up with a new slogan: "The $55 Haircut for a whole lot less." And we even trademarked "The $55 Haircut."

Danny designed a T-shirt that was sent to all certified Markham Style Innovator shops for their stylists to wear. We also provided an updated media kit around our new campaign. This included radio spots, ads for newspapers, brochures, and everything shop owners might need to promote "The $55 haircut for a whole lot less."

The idea was that you could get the same level of natural cut and style tailored for your head and face that I gave to my celebrity clients, but at a much lower cost. The shop owners and barbers loved the slogan, and our timing with the T-shirts was perfect. In fashion, designer labels were becoming more important than the actual clothes, and we'd found a way to put the Markham label on a haircut.

Shops started selling the shirts to their customers. As a result, everybody wanted to know about the $55 Haircut. It created lots of business for the local Markham shops and a ton of buzz for Markham Products nationwide. One article became syndicated and wound up in 44 different newspapers across the country, including the *Washington Post*.

As I continued to develop my biggest markets, I gave careful consideration to whom I could trust. When I thought about San Francisco, I remembered Patricia Fripp. I met her briefly when she was running Jay's San Francisco shop. She made a strong impression on me. Not only did I observe her skill behind the chair, but I could see that her management savvy was the reason that her Certified Markham Shop was so successful. She proved her eagerness and drive when, un-prompted, she flew to New York to observe me demonstrating on stage for three days at a big hair show.

I asked Patricia to come to Los Angeles to discuss becoming a Markham distributor and opening her own Markham Style Innovator shop. Over dinner, I made my pitch. "Patricia, you're one of the most talented stylists I've seen, and you've got the mind and drive to own your own place." I knew she was on track to open her own salon, and I wanted that salon to be part of the Markham brand.

The words were barely out of my mouth before Patricia, British and blonde, said, "You are absolutely right, and I'd love to be on the ground floor of what you're doing. I saw what you accomplished at Sebring."

Patricia had a sterling reputation, and she quickly became a Mark-ham distributor and self-financed the buyout of the business and lease of a longstanding barbershop in a prestigious building in the middle of San Francisco's financial district. She built out the space to her liking and hired a team of all female stylists. She ran Miss Fripp's Markham Style Innovator shop like a drill sergeant, all the while maintaining a pleasant and warm persona. Everything she did was regimented. Not only was she a great stylist herself, but she had a great mind for business.

Patricia made the most of every minute with her clients, which in-cluded some of the most powerful men in San Francisco. She taught her stylists to skip the idle chit-chat and spend the time instead talking to the client about the way his hair grew, whether it should be long or short to frame his face, and any concerns he had. She shared my belief that the time the customer is in that chair is an opportunity to educate him on the use of our products and to make their new cut and style look great.

Patricia was an A+ student and mastered the Markham Method. She helped her clients understand how their best features could be enhanced, like the eyes or smile, while deemphasizing less attractive features like the ears, all while using our certified cut, style, and products to achieve those results. Soon, her salon was one of the top salons in San Francisco.

Meanwhile, my trade shows and training events were growing in size, with audiences sometimes in the thousands. I needed someone else on stage with me who could demonstrate my method. Patricia became one of my all-star picks. She knew the business inside and out.

Convincing her to go on the road with me as a platform artist didn't take much. On stage, she hit all the right notes and often did the demos while I talked about what she was doing. She was especially good at teaching the concepts and showing how my technique could transform a man's looks.

Our contrasting speaking styles—her crisp British accent and my soft-spoken, Southwestern accent—complemented each other, too.

More importantly, Patricia understood the transformative power of the Markham brand. She pitched the concept as a form of self-improvement, explaining from the stage why caring for your hair properly can not only enhance your looks, but actually give you a whole new attitude in life. I was so impressed by her work ethic, dedication, continued drive, and commitment, I awarded her some Markham stock—she earned it! I also determined that if I ever had a job opening with an equally qualified female and male candidate, I'd give the job to the woman at equal pay. From my observation, women were generally more detail-oriented, more thorough, more rational, and they seemed to think through problems better than the men I'd known.

In the intervening years, Patricia has made quite a name for herself outside of the hair care industry as an in-demand executive speech coach, sales trainer, and multi-award-winning speaker. She became the first female president of the 3,600-member National Speakers Association and is the author or co-author of five books. In 2019, Patricia was named one of the Top 25 Women in Sales and Top 30 Coaching Gurus.

Takeaways

- With the right partner or team, even mistakes can be fun.
- Errors don't have to be fatal, as long as you move swiftly to correct them.
- Find solution-oriented people who enjoy a challenge.
- Lead, don't follow.
- Reward good, dedicated people.

INGREDIENT #10

EVERYBODY MATTERS

J ust as I was launching Markham Products, my ex-wife Janet got married for the third time and called me with shocking news. "Jim, my new husband wants to adopt Vickie and Bobby. He wants to be a real father to them," she said. "I think it's confusing for you to be in their life."

It felt like déjà vu. "What are you talking about, Janet?" I said. "I come see Vickie and Bobby every time I'm in Farmington. They're everything to me."

Once again, the words stung. "I've made up my mind, Jim. You can't stop it. They are going to be baptized in the church and sealed to him for all eternity."

"No matter what you do, you can't change the fact that I'm their father," I said. "I am coming to see them. I want to hear it from them."

I flew to Farmington to talk to Vickie, who was 12, and Bobby, 10 at the time. They stopped me in my tracks and echoed their mother's words. "Are you sure this is what you really want?" I finally asked each of them individually, staring into their eyes.

Bobby, his shoulders slumped, avoided looking at me. Vickie tried to hide behind a tremulous smile.

They both nodded yes slowly. Big tears slid down their cheeks. I told both of them that I'd always love them no matter what their last name was, and I'd always be there for them.

I remembered all the times Vickie would cry out as a toddler whenever her mother would kick me out: "Daddy, please don't leave me."

I'd always tell her, "I'll be back for you."

As painful as it was, I hugged them both tightly. I whispered those words in Vickie's ears, hoping she'd remember those words from long ago that I always kept that promise. Her sky-blue eyes widened and filled with fresh tears.

Then I left, uncertain of whether my relationship with my children was irretrievably broken. All I knew was that I would never give up on loving them. I made the long drive back to Albuquerque and returned to LA with a shattered heart.

I threw myself back into my work. That's the only way I knew how to cope. Once I was up and running with Markham Products, my celebrity clientele quickly returned. I was again taking care of major stars like Robert Redford, Lee Marvin, Paul Anka, Andy Williams, James Garner, and Steve McQueen.

After Paul Newman gave me my first opportunity to work with him on a film, he tapped me to work with him on almost every film he made through the early 1980s. I never charged him for my services. Instead, I made sure he was well supplied with Markham Products, always shipping them to his movie sets and homes. Through the years, what I got from Paul was worth far more than anything he might have paid me: He taught me how to live a meaningful life.

Paul stood apart from all the other celebrities I'd worked with, not just because of his star power, but because he was genuine and kind. Once, when I was in Tucson, Arizona, while he was filming *The Life and Times of Judge Roy Bean*, he came to my hotel room for a cut. He took one look at the water stains on the walls in the small room and said, "Markham, I'm leaving tonight for New York, you can just take my room."

After I was done with his cut, I followed him up to his room, which turned out to be a very large hotel suite, decorated like his home in LA.

He must have noticed my surprise, as I eyed the beautiful china in the dining room table. "I'm on the road for many months at a time. Living like this helps me feel at home."

He ordered an early dinner for us and then asked, "What do you know about wine?"

"Not much," I admitted. There was never any reason to pretend around Paul. He treated everyone with equal respect.

Paul preferred red wines, mostly Italian and vintage French wines. He pulled out a bottle from his personal collection and showed me the label. A warm smile came over his face as he popped open the cork, "This is a real good one," he said. "We've got to let it breathe." A true connoisseur, he loved to talk about the finish and the characteristics of the wine. This one was a 1968 Chateau Margaux. At the time, the bottle was worth about maybe $700–$800. Today, it's priceless.

That was my wine lesson. And from that day on, every time I cut Paul's hair, he would send me home with one or two bottles of his new favorite wines.

The message that Paul communicated to me through his actions was that everything matters—especially how you treat others. Part of Paul's charm was that he was genuinely interested in people. He was curious and asked lots of questions. More importantly, he listened to the answers. He paid attention to the details. He cared.

Paul also taught me that part of living a good life is being thoughtful about what you do for yourself, too. Until seeing Paul's suite, I'd never given any thought to examining what refueled me. I'd never had the luxury of self-reflection because I'd been functioning in survival mode my entire life. The last several years, I'd been busy running and gunning around the country with Sebring and now Markham. But Paul explained that becoming depleted helps no one. It was eye-opening to see the value he put on creating a peaceful, beautiful space. I learned many things from Paul, including how to create a real home for myself, no matter where I landed—a lesson I learned from him that I still value to this day.

Whether Paul was on the road or at home, I'd travel to maintain his regular appointment. One day, while cutting his hair in the living room, his wife Joanne entered through the kitchen door. Paul suddenly jumped out of the chair and threw off his smock. He took the dry cleaning from Joanne and laid it on a nearby chair. Then he swept her into his arms and planted a kiss on her lips and said, "Hello, lovely lady. I missed you."

Wow, if that's how an international sex symbol treats his wife, how much more should a mere mortal like me be doing? No wonder my first two marriages flopped.

Joanne had only been gone about an hour, but I could tell Paul wasn't putting on a show for my sake. This was the real man—courteous, romantic, and respectful. I'd never witnessed another couple behave this way. For the first time in my life, I was getting a front-row seat on what a healthy marriage looked like.

Paul steadily built his legend with me—without even trying. I no longer thought about his celebrity so much as the giant he was as a man, who loved his wife and his children fiercely and wasn't afraid to show it. He was the kind of individual worth imitating. The polar opposite of all the violent, broken men I'd encountered throughout my childhood. I never told Paul, but I came to view him not only as a mentor, but somewhat as a father figure.

With behind-the-scenes access to celebrity lives, I'd learned how quickly things could go south if they didn't manage themselves well. This became especially key when a competitor tried to sabotage their careers. Once again, I learned from Paul the importance of staying above the fray.

I never once heard Paul say anything negative about anyone. He only spoke kindly of people and focused on the good. He was gracious with fans as well as his colleagues. The only time I ever saw him get irritated was once when he was trying to eat a sandwich and fans kept interrupting him at dinner, but even then, he kept his cool.

Don't get me wrong, Paul was fiercely competitive. He loved to win, but he didn't fight dirty. He kept his own counsel and understood that when you can't hold your tongue it reflects badly on you.

He taught me that the best strategy to employ when we hear that someone is talking bad about us is to listen to the criticism to see if there's even a hint of truth in it.

On the other hand, if the negative talk is completely off base, ignore it. I've heard all kinds of crazy stuff about myself over the years. I've even had people lay claim to my accomplishments. But thanks to Paul, I've chosen to let my actions do the talking for me.

For the most part, I try to avoid anything negative—especially litigation.

In the hair business, we get close to our clients. They trust us with their image, and it's our job to make them look good and feel good. When they sit in the chair, they tend to relax and share their most private thoughts. It's crucial to keep their secrets confidential and give them the respect we'd want for ourselves.

When I owned Markham Products, my office was housed in a 30-story modern office building on Wilshire Boulevard. We were on the twelfth floor, and though I rarely did cuts in the office, I kept a barber's chair there just in case. One day, Paul asked if he could stop by for a cut. Within five minutes of the star's arrival, nearly every woman in the building was storming our suite. We had to double-lock the door and call building security to intervene.

I felt terrible about the chaos, but Paul was unfazed. After I finished his cut, he smiled and said, "Markham, I'm assuming there's got to be a better way out than the way I came in."

Luckily, I knew of a private elevator. He was able to give his fans the slip, but women were offering me as much as $500 for a lock of his hair, an offer I would have never even considered because I've always valued my clients more than I value money.

In time, my relationship with Paul grew into a genuine friendship. In fact, years later when film editor Bob Wyman saw the autographed photos of Paul on my wall, he seemed surprised. "What you've got here is really rare," he said, noting that Paul had signed some of them P.L. Newman, which stood for Paul Leonard. "He only signs with his initials for his family and real close friends."

It was nice to learn that Paul had valued our friendship as much as I had. Recently, I'd learned from his daughter Clea that Paul had kept Markham Products in all of his homes. "Everybody in our family used them," she said. "I still remember how the cherry almond shampoo smelled. Whenever I smell that scent, I think of Pops."

While I was given access to the private lives of many celebrities like Paul, no amount of money was worth risking my relationship with the clients I cut and styled. I understood that they, like anyone else, prefer to do business with people they trust.

With Markham's success, and a larger marketing budget, Danny and I hired Mahoney/Wasserman & Associates, a top public relations agency that handled Johnny Carson. They gave us the star treatment — pitching me to newspapers, magazines, radio, and TV stations all over the country.

After one of many appearances demonstrating the Markham styling technique on Regis Philbin's *AM Los Angeles*, I received a call from Johnny Carson. "I saw your work," he said. "I'd like to make an appointment."

Johnny initially insisted on coming to my office, but like with Paul Newman, his presence created such a stir that we met at his house. Quiet and reserved, Johnny was always on time and paid me $100 a cut, which he scheduled for every two and a half weeks like clockwork.

My clients were at the top of their game. Sure, there may have been an element of luck for some of them, but nearly all of the celebrities I've ever known have worked hard at their craft and equally hard at preserving their image.

Establishing that kind of reputation and trust with my clients required understanding where the boundaries are. I was always careful to remain professional above all else. I'd learned from the sale of Sebring how abruptly my entry card into that world could be pulled. I took nothing for granted.

About this time, I met Wolfman Jack, a famous disc jockey and a real character. The first time I ever cut Wolfman's hair, Steve McQueen dropped by the office, asking if I could squeeze him in. "Sure," I said. "As soon as I finish Wolfman."

Minutes later, Academy Award-winning tough guy Lee Marvin entered the salon. I could sense Wolfman getting uncomfortable at the growing line of celebrities waiting for the chair he was occupying.

The next time I saw him, he brought it up. "I've never seen so many of my screen idols in one place, Jim," he said. "That was crazy, man. I can't believe you made those kind of guys wait, so you could cut my hair."[1]

"Everybody matters," I said, drawing on the lessons Paul had taught me.

After that, Wolfman and I got along famously. I even invited him to attend several Markham shows with me, and we began traveling together like I had for a few years with Peter Lawford when I'd first started Markham. Despite his wild reputation, he proved to be a loyal and trustworthy collaborator, and I hired him to do many TV and radio spots for Markham Products.

Takeaways

- Stay above the fray. Don't contribute to negativity.

- Never favor one client over another. Everybody deserves our best.

- Respect healthy boundaries.

- People prefer to do business with people they trust.

- Guard others' privacy and never betray a confidence.

- Avoid gossip.

GALLERY

Jim Markham as an infant with
older brother Bill and sister Betty

Jim at age 12

Jim holding daughter Vickie and
wife Janet holding son Robert in 1962

Jay Sebring with Jim right after they'd given each other
haircuts taken at Jim's Sebring International Salon in
Albuquerque in July 1969
—the last known image of Jay prior to his murder

Sebring International Salon, Los Angeles, 1970. From Jim's publicity shoot in front of Sebring International with his publicist on the left and photographer on the right

Jim's first publicity headshot upon arrival to
Hollywood when he took over Sebring International

Women's World

Tate, Sebring Parents Help Launch Successor

By JOAN KAISER
—World-Examiner Beauty Editor

"We are relieved." There were no gleaming smiles wreathing the faces of Mr. and Mrs. Leonard Kummer (parents of the slain Jay Sebring) or Col. and Mrs. Paul Tate (U.S.A. ret.), parents of Sharon Tate, as they remarked on Los Angeles police department announcements on arrests made in the Tate-Sebring murders.

Arrests won't bring either couple's child back but this week's sensational disclosures have helped erase some of the unpleasant rumors circulating about their personal life styles.

The arrests couldn't have come at a more ironic time; if there is such a thing where murder is concerned. For Jay Sebring's successor was named this week and the uncertain cloud hovering over Sebring International looked a little less grim Tuesday night when Peter Lawford hosted the announcement party at The Factory.

Sebring's business heir is 26 - year - old Jim Markham, owner of Sebring's first franchised shop in Albuquerque, New Mexico, for the past two years.

Kummer, under Sebring's will, is now Chairman of the Board of Sebring, Inc. He came from Detroit for the introduction event, joining John Madden, president, and Lawford as hosts.

Lawford, a long-time friend of Jay's, had been a model in a 2½-hour training film Sebring made just prior to his death. Although most refuse to allow their names to be given, rumor is he is a Sebring stockholder as well, along with Herb Alpert, the Paul Newmans, Victor Lounes of London and other unidentified Hollywood personalities.

The slight, soft-spoken

Markham knew Sebring and of his plans to train barbers in his techniques so that a man could travel any place in the world and receive the same type of haircut.

While Markham spoke, a jeweled ankh ring flashed from his left hand. Since Sebring chose a redesigned ankh as his firm's symbol the ring had more than passing significance.

"No one knows just why Jay picked an ankh," Markham remarked. "It was a sign of enduring life in Egyptian art (a tau cross with a loop at the top in the design shape) and has become the hippies' international symbol of love."

Markham made his ring, taking 14 months to research and sculpt it in gold. On its sides are reliefs of King Tutankhamen, the 14th century B.C. pharoh who used the ankh as a symbol, Egyptian hieroglyphics, falcon-headed figures and other carvings.

Jim Markham, new president of Sebring International, with Mr. and Mrs. Leonard Kummer, parents of Jay Sebring.

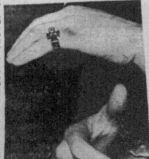

A jeweled ankh ring worn by Jim Markham, patterned after a redesigned ankh Sebring selected as his firm's symbol.

The late Jay Sebring's parents launch Jim Markham as their son's successor

Paul Newman with the producer/director John Foreman
from *Sometimes a Great Notion*

Actor Paul Newman—*Butch Cassidy and the Sundance Kid*, 1969

Actor Paul Newman—*Butch Cassidy and the Sundance Kid*, 1969

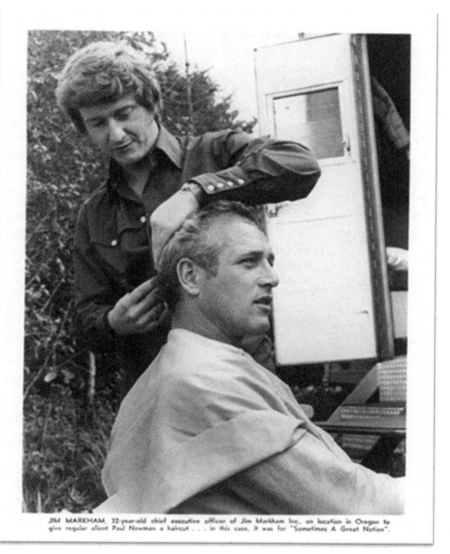

JIM MARKHAM, 32-year-old chief executive officer of Jim Markham Inc., on location in Oregon to give regular client Paul Newman a haircut . . . in this case, it was for "Sometimes A Great Notion".

For his work on *Sometimes a Great Notion*,
Jim became the first barber to ever receive film credit

PAUL NEWMAN

March 16, 1971

Dear Jim:

    It's nice to know that
Jay Sebring's shop is going strong
under your aegis and to find it's
still a first-class operation.

    I shall tout it to the
guys wherever possible. Ladies
too.

Best,

Paul Newman

PLN:ms

Mr. Jim Markham
725 North Fiarfax
Hollywood, California 90046

Letter to Jim from Paul Newman

Paul Newman and Lee Marvin on the set of *Pocket Money*

PAUL NEWMAN

March 11, 1976

Mr. Jim Markham
6300 Wilshire Blvd.
Suite 1201
Los Angeles, Calif.   90068

Dear Jim:

     Just to make things a matter of public
record, I am grateful for all the cooperation you
have given in far away places, outrageous hours
above and beyond the call of duty to keep this
poor head in shape.

     If you want to apologize, I will be in
your room.

             Yours,

PN:bs

Letter #2 to Jim from Paul Newman

Paul Newman publicity photo from *Buffalo Bill and the Indians*
with the rare P.L. signature, which stood for Paul Leonard
and was reserved for family and close friends

Actor Steve McQueen—*Bullitt*, 1968

One of the many promotions
Peter Lawford did for Markham Products

Jim and his client Peter Lawford, who invested
in Markham Products and served as a spokesman

Jim and his spokesman Peter Lawford promoting Markham Style
Innovator Shops and Markham Products

Michael Sarrazin and Jim Markham
on the set of *Sometimes a Great Notion*

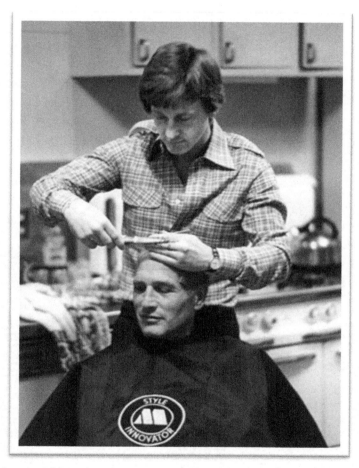

Jim Markham and actor Paul Newman in Paul's home in
Beverly Hills prepping for a feature in the *Washington Post*

Former *Tonight Show* host for 30 years, Johnny Carson

WOLFMAN JACK

Long-time client and Markham pitchman Wolfman Jack
remained a loyal friend throughout his life

Freddie Prinze

Dennis Weaver

James Garner

Michael Benjamin

Richard Jaekel

Peter Lupus

Kerry Berk Edelman with husband Bobby
and sons Mychal and Bryan Edelman in 1997

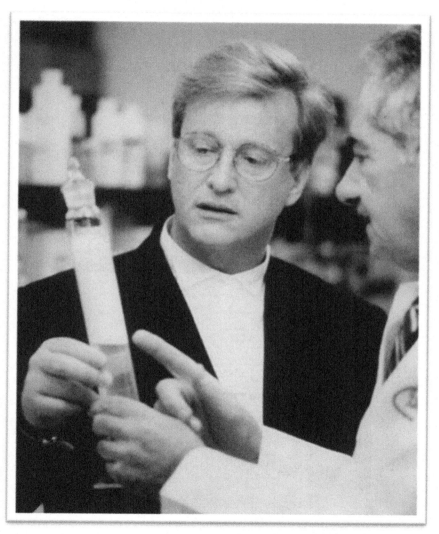

Jim working on product development in the lab with his chemist

Style

Profile

A Hair Mogul's Manson Memories: 'I Thought I Was Next'

Joe Markham, stylist to Paul Newman and Steve McQueen, hosted a federal sting to uncover the motives behind the murders and now shares his alternative belief 'I never bought into the race war theory.' By Tatiana Siegel

Jim Markham remembers vividly the days following the grisly Manson murders of Roman Polanski's pregnant wife, Sharon Tate, her former boyfriend and hairstylist Jay Sebring and three others at the director's Benedict Canyon residence in August 1969. At the time, Markham was Sebring's protégé and business partner in a budding franchise of men's hair salons that stretched from a star-packed outpost on the corner of L.A.'s Melrose and Fairfax to Miami. Sebring became the second person to die at the hands of the Manson family members during an infamous killing spree that claimed seven lives, including coffee heiress Abigail Folger and her lover, Polish screenwriter Wojciech Frykowski.

Markham, then 15 and splitting his time between his hometown of Albuquerque, New Mexico, and L.A., was the heir apparent to Sebring's 400-plus clientele, which included Paul Newman, Frank Sinatra and Steve McQueen. Markham heard the news on the radio and got on the phone with Sebring International president John Madden. "Jay and I had talked many times ... that I'd be his successor if anything ever happened to him," Markham recalls. "I just took right over out of necessity."

The hair-care mogul sipped a Perrier on the deck of the Majestic Hotel in Cannes when he met with THR, a day after the world premiere of Once Upon a Time in Hollywood — Quentin Tarantino's spin on the events surrounding the Charles Manson-directed murders. (In the movie, Sebring is a key character played by Emile Hirsch.) By Markham's side was his wife of 33 years, Cheryl — the daughter of Don Genis, special effects guru behind Star Wars — who came of age during the Manson era.

Revisiting the weeks that followed the killings is both painful and cathartic for Markham, now 75 and fabulously wealthy thanks to founding four hair-care companies, including Pureology Serious Colour Care, which he sold to L'Oréal in 2007 for $280 million. (He pocketed more than $100 million on that deal alone.) Markham has never talked in detail about his entanglement in the infamous investigation that captured headlines worldwide and continues to fascinate new generations. His tale reveals his previously unknown role in the critical months after the murders, as law enforcement attempted to identify the killers and decipher their motives with no break in the case.

Days after the murders, and at the behest of Sebring's father, Markham began living at the house where he had been a frequent guest. Sebring's Bavarian-style home, once owned by Jean Harlow and located on Easton Drive in Beverly Hills — just one mile away from the Polanski-Tate residence on Cielo Drive. "I'm living in Jay's house with raccoons on the roof — it would sound like somebody walking on the top of the house," he says. "I finally had to move out. I thought I was going to be next. They hadn't caught Manson. Nobody knew why it happened."

As Markham remembers, Tate's father, a count in Army intelligence, began working with federal agents on the investigation. The agents told Markham that they believed the killers were connected to the salon (murder victim Folger also had a connection to the hair enterprise given that she was an investor in Sebring International). The salon was bugged, but ultimately that line of inquiry lost steam. Once the Manson Family became suspects, however, about six months after the murders, he feels enlisted a willing Markham to set up a sting at his rented Brentwood home. He was to host a meeting between a woman and a man she had met at a hair, someone who had recounted to her at length how he had met Manson in

Photographed by Fabrizio Maltese

Hollywood Reporter story on *Once Upon a Time in Hollywood* and the Manson murders

Uncle Earl Kamakaonaona Regidor, Manager, Ka'upulehu Cultural
Center, at home blessing with daughter Vickie Markham-Larson,
Jim, wife Cheryl Markham, sons Robert and Jay Markham

Mary Rector, Vidal Sassoon, Jim Markham and Michael
O'Rourke participating in Hairdressers Unlocking Hope
in support of Habitat for Humanity after Hurricane Katrina

2007 Ernst & Young Regional Entrepreneur of the Year
for Consumer Retail Products

Jim and wife Cheryl accepting their award
as City of Hope Honorees

Jim's five-decade career is recognized by presenting him the 2019 Intercoiffure Lifetime Achievement Icon Award

INGREDIENT #11

YOU CAN'T
SAVE EVERYBODY

I t had been four years since I'd launched my namesake company, Markham Products. Christmas was around the corner, and I suddenly felt nudged to visit my mother. I hadn't been back home for the holidays in years—not that we'd ever really celebrated.

As I reached the outskirts of Hobbs, luminarias lined the flat roofs and driveways. The lights shone beautifully, marking the town with a magical holiday spirit, but for me, they brought a sad reminder of the many childhood Christmases that had gone uncelebrated. I rarely allowed myself a melancholy moment, but those painful memories brought heavy emotions to me.

My brother, his wife, and kids now lived near Mom in Hobbs. Dad had come into town to stay with Bobby for the holidays, and I'd planned to stay at Mom's current place. I wasn't sure how long she'd been in this rental. She had a new boyfriend by that point—yet another alcoholic—who'd been living with her for a while. Mom met me on the front porch. She immediately wrapped me in a big hug and then clapped her hands in delight.

"I'm so glad you're here!" she said. "I made all your favorites: fried chicken, mashed potatoes and gravy with cornbread. And for dessert, I've got pies—pumpkin, apple, and cherry."

The comforting smells coming from the kitchen brought back the few good memories I had from growing up. "Thanks, Mom," I said, assuring her I'd found no better food than hers no matter how far I'd roamed. As we made our way into the house, I was comforted to find she still went out of her way to keep everything neat and tidy. Regardless of her financial strains, she knew how to make a house a home.

When I took my luggage up to my room, I caught my breath. There, taped on the wall, were every single one of the newspaper clippings and magazine articles I'd sent her over the years. I was overcome with emotion. Tears came to my eyes, but I shut my eyes tightly. I had cried so much as a child that I never wanted to shed another tear.

All that time, I didn't think she cared at all, but the evidence was undeniable. She was proud of me. For all her shortcomings, she'd gone all out to make my homecoming feel special.

After dinner, the entire family sat in the tiny living room; everybody was laughing and talking. It was sunny and brisk on Christmas.

Mom wasn't drinking, and I didn't dare drink a drop, fearful of encouraging her old destructive habit. Mom's boyfriend scarcely said a word to anyone. Instead, he sat in the corner drinking beer the entire evening.

At one point, Mom told everyone about visiting me in Hollywood. "Jim drove me all around the city in his fancy wheels, didn't you, Jimbo?"

I jumped in to tell the others about my Mercedes 450 SL.

Suddenly, a familiar expression flashed across my father's face— anger, bitterness, jealousy or maybe a mix of all three. "Well, I just paid $100,000 for a new truck, and you don't hear me bragging about it." He glared straight at me with a cold, intimidating stare. "I hope you don't look down on the good people of this town. They're salt-of-the-earth folk, and you're no better than any of 'em."

His words stung and all those old doubts crept back to haunt me. *Maybe I'm too full of myself.* But then my temper flared, too, because I remembered all the times Dad had refused to acknowledge any of my achievements. I had longed to hear him say the words: *I am proud of you, son*—about something, anything. But that never happened. Ever.

After an awkward moment, I suppressed my anger and said, "Of course not, Dad. I could never forget my roots."

Eventually, the tension evaporated, and everybody went back to talking as if we were one big happy family. And for that one night, I guess we were.

Dad, Bobby, and the others left around 10:00 p.m. on Christmas Eve, leaving Mom and me alone in the living room. She sat next to me on the sofa and asked, "Jimbo, do you think you could get Janet to let Vickie and Bobby come stay with me for a few weeks next summer? I'd dearly love to see them."

"I'd love that, Mom. Of course, you'd need to stay sober. For the next six months, at least. I can't bring them into the kind of chaos I knew as a child."

"I understand, Jim. I promise. I can do it. You're gonna be so surprised."

"Sure you can do it, Mom. I believe in you," I said, trying to encourage her, but on the inside I remained doubtful she could really live up to that promise—especially with the latest boyfriend drinking his way through the holidays, ready to drag her back to her old ways.

Emotionally exhausted after just one day back in Hobbs, I collapsed right there on the couch. I knew I faced a long night of insomnia. Too many memories were flooding back—and few of them were good.

In silence, Mom gave me a maternal hug. She seemed to sense that despite all I'd achieved since leaving home, what I needed most was to feel loved, to be given the reassurance of a mother's nurturing touch.

We didn't talk, but in the quiet of the house I felt the hot core of anger slowly start to melt away. In my heart, I forgave her for all the times she'd left me unprotected, for abandoning me over and over again when I was young and vulnerable and in need of a safe place to call home. I forgave myself too, letting go of the guilt I'd long carried for being helpless to save her from many demons.

In that moment, I knew without a doubt that my mother, although deeply flawed, loved me as best she could.

I spent the first day of Memorial Day Weekend 1977 partying at Steve McQueen's beach house. I returned home late that night to a blinking message light on my answering machine. I punched the button, and my mother's voice was shrieking at me: "Jim, Jim, he's gonna kill me. He's gonna kill me this time." She was slurring her words before the message ended.

Two more messages followed, each with the even more fear and urgency in her voice.

About that time, my phone rang. It was my brother. "Mom's been shot," he said. "You better get here quick if you want to see her."

I immediately flew into Roswell, New Mexico, where I rented a car and raced the rest of the way to Hobbs.

As I feared, Mom had fallen off the wagon, and she and her boyfriend had tangled in an argument. During the fight, she'd managed to lock him out of the house, but he shot through the door, hitting Mom, who'd been standing against the door to block his entrance. It then sliced through her femoral artery just above her leg. In a panic, her boyfriend waited about 45 minutes before calling the police and telling them what he'd done. By the time she reached the hospital, she'd already lost an enormous amount of blood.

When the nurse hustled me in to see my mother, she was clinging to life. Her eyes were open, but she was paralyzed and couldn't speak. "It's okay, Mama, I'm here," I whispered, smoothing her thin blonde hair as tears spilled from my eyes. "I'm here." I'd barely gotten the words out when she flatlined.

There was a flood of panic as I was hustled out of the way. The doctor tried desperately to resuscitate her. I hadn't prayed much since my first divorce, but in that moment, I asked God to give Mama a chance.

"Hang on, Mama," I begged. "Vickie and Bobby are on their way. Please, hang on."

Amazingly, after far-too-many rounds of CPR, she began to show a pulse again. The doctor exhaled. Then, he looked at me with heavy eyes and said, "She's not going to make it much longer."

Vickie and Bobby arrived at the hospital from Farmington shortly before 5 p.m. Saturday night. Just as Vickie walked through the door of the hospital room with Bobby right on her heels, Mama, with tears in her eyes, took one last breath and left this world. The beep of that awful machine signaled that she was gone the moment Bobby entered the room. She was only 61 when she was buried on Memorial Day.

When I went to her house, the small guest rooms were neat and orderly, all prepared for the grandchildren's first visit with her, an arrangement that had been scheduled for the following month.

For years, I'd scarcely slept, fearing that this day was coming. I'd spent my entire life being tortured by nightmares over and over again, in which I came close to saving my mom, but could never quite reach her in time. No matter how the scenario played out in my dreams, I was never enough. Never strong enough, never big enough, never fast enough. But this time, the nightmare had become a reality and my Mama was gone.

Much as I grieved, I was especially haunted by the knowledge of what could have happened if my children had been in her house at that time.

My mind circled back through our last visit, when I'd come home for Christmas and she'd held me on the sofa. I'd taken real comfort in that moment between us when I was wrapped in her embrace, letting the waves of forgiveness and love pass over us. I knew she was proud of me. I knew she loved me. I knew she was sorry for all she'd done to hurt me, even if the words had never been said.

I'd built my career on finding answers to problems and creating wonderful products to make people feel good about themselves, but I couldn't heal my mother's fractured sense of self. I felt like I was watching her drown in slow motion—a drowning that had been happening my entire life.

But by nothing less than miraculous timing, I'd been given that chance to forgive her and to forgive myself. And to know that, in the end, I was enough. I'd always been enough. And that Mom's struggles had never been my fault.

As terrible and traumatic as my mom's death had been, a strange gift came from that devastating loss. I reconnected with my children, Vickie and Bobby. We left the hospital together. It was the first time I'd been with them in so long, and we talked and talked.

They both attended her funeral and were devastated to have lost their grandmother so close to the time they were finally going to get to know her. We grieved deeply together, and I realized that maybe Mom was watching over all of us. She'd been pulling for them all their lives. She'd always say, "Don't you forget those kids. They will need you."

Takeaways

- You can't always save the people you love.

- Forgiveness sets you free.

- Miracles do happen.

- Love never dies.

- We can't repair the damage someone else has done to themselves but we can take steps to heal ourselves and strengthen our relationships.

INGREDIENT #12

LIFE IS SWEETER
WHEN SHARED

As a busy entrepreneur building my company, I tried to look beyond the harsh realities I'd already known—especially where relationships were concerned. After such a turbulent childhood, plus two divorces before the age of 22, I hadn't been eager to let anyone get too close.

During my Markham Products days, I'd casually been dating models and starlets, avoiding any serious entanglements. It was the mid to late '70s, and like many successful people in Los Angeles, I'd been enjoying the party life. *Cosmopolitan* magazine had even named me as one of the finalists for most eligible bachelor. I'd also allowed my hectic travel schedule and company obligations consume me. In a nutshell, I was having too much fun being free to focus on any kind of serious relationship.

Until one day when I got a call from my ex, Janet: "Jim, I'm having a problem with Vickie. She wants to go to beauty school, and I thought maybe she could come out there and be with you."

My heart began to race. After all these years with only sporadic phone calls and a few visits permitted by my ex, I was finally being given the chance to be the dad I'd always hoped to be. I was elated, but nervous. "Beauty school? That's great news! I'll send you the money for a plane ticket," I said. "We'll figure it out."

By that point in time, I'd trained countless students and professionals in the hair industry, but this one was going to be a challenge. This time it wasn't just my future at stake. It was my 17-year-old daughter's.

Jittery with excitement, I paced at the gate, waiting for Vickie to come off the flight. I couldn't stop smiling when I spotted my beautiful daughter. Her white-blonde hair crowned her like a halo, with a long, feathered cut, similar to Farrah Fawcett's. She wore embroidered bellbottom jeans and a halter top.

Aside from my mom's funeral, I'd hardly seen Vickie for any significant length of time. She may have had a new last name, but she was still my girl and now I had a chance to make her feel secure in that.

"Hi, Dad," she said, almost casually in a confident voice, as if we'd just seen each other the other day.

I wrapped her in a hug, and she held on tight, just like she did when she was a little girl. "I'm really glad you're here, honey. I think you're going to like Los Angeles," I said. "What would you like to see while you're here?"

"Well, first I want to see your office," she said, picking up the pace. "And the Hollywood sign and the Pacific Ocean. I've never seen the ocean."

Smiling, I draped one arm around her small shoulders. I remembered all those same firsts when I arrived to the city from the desert. It felt like a lifetime had passed since then.

I retrieved her suitcase and led her to the parking garage.

"No way! This is your car?" Her eyes grew wide as she ran her hand over to my sapphire blue Mercedes-Benz.

I put her suitcase into the trunk. "You don't think I stole it, do you?" I teased. "You can make a nice living in the hair business if you work hard. Don't worry. I'll teach you everything I know, honey."

She beamed, and I couldn't believe how much she looked like her mother.

"I've already gotten you signed up for beauty school in Beverly Hills, honey. You'll start next week."

"Thank you." She said, "I'm so excited." Then with a dramatic sigh, she added, "You have no idea how bad I wanted to get out of Farmington."

I gave her a wink. "Oh, I think I might know that feeling a little bit."

Just like that, I'd become a single dad. I was overjoyed to have Vickie in my home. But the truth was, I'd been living the bachelor life for a long-time and being thrust into this role after more than five years of alienation, certainly demanded a lot of adjustments for both of us. Although Vickie and I got along surprisingly well, the one sticking point for my daughter was my active dating life. She made it clear she was not a fan of the parade of women who floated in and out of my house.

Two months after Vickie moved in with me, her frustration came to a head over dinner at her favorite Mexican restaurant, El Coyote. We were celebrating her success at beauty school when she blindsided me by asking, "Why do you date all those bimbos, Dad?"

I fired back, "Why can't you be nice to any of the women I bring around?"

"Because the girls you date are all so weird," she argued. "Don't you know any nice girls?" She emphasized the word *nice*.

The dinner didn't go as I'd hoped, and I was defensive for the rest of the evening. Once we got home, she went to her room and slammed the door, clearly disgusted with me. I pulled out my little black book, determined to prove her wrong. But the more I looked, the more I realized my daughter was right. Perhaps I really didn't know any *nice* girls.

Finally, I came across the number of a girl I'd met. She was the daughter of a man who owned one of the top Hollywood special effects companies. Her name was Cheryl Genis.

Over the years, we'd often played tennis with a group of friends, and had occasionally gone to breakfast together. She was smart, pretty, and loved to laugh. But I'd never asked her out because I was nine years older than her, divorced, and had three kids.

I worried the age difference might prove to be a problem, especially because she was only seven years older than my daughter. But she was the only "nice" girl who interested me, so the next day I dialed Cheryl's number and hoped for the best.

"Hi, Cheryl, this is Jim Markham." I tried to sound confident, even though I was feeling uncharacteristically nervous. "I wondered if you'd be available to join me for dinner? Tomorrow night?"

She started laughing and said, "Are you asking me out on a date . . . *with you?*"

Clearly, this had been a mistake, but it was too late to turn back now. "Yeah, I think I am."

She paused. *Not a good sign.* But then she said, "Well, okay."

"Okay?" I said, half surprised she'd agreed. "Um. . . I'll be bringing my daughter with me. That okay?"

"Wonderful! I'll look forward to meeting her," she said.

The next evening, Vickie and I dressed to impress and rode together to pick up Cheryl from her condo in Studio City. From there, I drove us all to dinner at the Fish Shanty on La Cienega in Beverly Hills. Soon, the three of us were talking, and just having a good time. One thing was for sure, this was nothing like any of the times I'd attempted to introduce Vickie to any of my girlfriends.

The two of them acted like they'd known each other for years. There was an ease to their relationship that just felt right, and I couldn't have been more relieved. After dinner, Cheryl came back to the house with us and Vickie went to her room, leaving us alone.

I'd long been impressed by Cheryl's ambition and intellect. Over the many times we'd shared as friends, she'd always asked interesting questions about my profession and my days at Sebring. At the time, she was working at her mother's interior design firm. That evening, we talked about her love for cinema and her ambition to be a set designer. Because she'd grown up with two entrepreneurs and her dad was acclaimed in the business, she was accustomed to being around movie stars and had a much clearer grasp of what I did than most of the other women I'd dated.

I poured two glasses of wine and turned on my sound system. I casually played Fleetwood Mac's *Rumours* album. The sparks between us took both of us by surprise, and that flicker quickly grew into a fire.

My daughter had been right. All those years, I'd been looking for love in the wrong places. Once Cheryl came into my life, she never left.

If I hadn't put myself in the position to repair my relationship with Vickie, I likely never would have realized that the woman destined to be my life-long partner had been right under my nose all the time.

Shortly into our relationship, Cheryl got a call from the head of props at Universal Studios. He explained that he was retiring and was on his last week at the job. Every month for the previous two years, she'd checked in with him to see if there were any openings, which she'd done with every movie studio in town. But like most people trying to enter the film industry, Cheryl had been caught between a rock and a hard place. She didn't have a Screen Actors Guild (SAG) card, so nobody would give her the opportunity. To be eligible for SAG, you had to have worked in the industry.

He told Cheryl, "In all my years, I've never met anyone more persistent than you. You know what, girl? I'm hiring you."

She started the next day, leaving our place by 6:00 a.m. in order to be on the studio lot by 7:00. She didn't leave work until 9:00 at night. Her five-day-a-week schedule was brutal, and they often asked her to work overtime and extra days. She was one of the few women in props or set design at any of the studios. Still, she loved the work, and I was proud of her landing her dream job.

About two months into it, I invited Cheryl to accompany me to a hair convention in Las Vegas. We both loved Vegas—the shows, blackjack, the energy. When I told her the dates, she became depressed. "I'm scheduled to work," she said.

That night she was restless in bed, and I was awake with insomnia, as usual. "I don't know what to do," Cheryl confessed. "I've always dreamt of designing sets, but now that I've gotten the job, I'm not sure I want it."

"You don't like the work?" I asked, concerned that something might have happened at the job.

"No, I love it," she insisted. "But I don't know… I guess I didn't realize how consuming it would become. It doesn't really allow me any time for myself."

I took her hand and listened as she worked through the pros and cons. Then I said, "Sometimes what we think we want doesn't work out the way we expected."

"Would you think I was a loser if I quit?" she asked.

"No, not at all," I said, surprised she was considering leaving the job. "If anything, it would just tell me that you've successfully identified something that you don't want to do. There's never any shame in learning more about ourselves. That's growing, not quitting."

She was quiet for a while, then she said, "The direction I want to go is the same as you. That's what I want."

Taking her hand in mine, I pulled her closer. "I'm with you, Cheryl. But I don't want you to give up your dreams for mine. There's room for both of us to succeed."

"I've made up my mind," she said. "I'll resign tomorrow and go back to work with Mom's design firm. That's what I really want."

I held her tight and said, "Las Vegas, here we come."

Cheryl's mother, Arline, was happy to have her daughter back working at her busy firm. The job also helped to feed Cheryl's creative hunger. I'd never met another woman like Cheryl. She was fiercely loyal to me and seemed committed to our relationship for the long haul. This was a first for me, and I too was in it with my whole heart.

When we bought a house together in Woodland Hills, her mother's attitude toward me suddenly shifted. My appearance on *The Dating Game* while Cheryl and I were living together probably didn't help my case, as it added to my reputation as a playboy. Despite Arline's concerns, Cheryl assured me she felt secure in our relationship. We were inseparable, and she understood my fast reputation was just part of the image. We'd been faithful to one another from the start and we were very happy as partners.

Her mother was another matter. Until we'd purchased the house together, Arline had been supportive of our relationship. But once we took the major step toward our future together, she suddenly seemed afraid of how deeply entwined our lives had become.

This new shift in Arline's attitude was uncomfortable for Cheryl since they worked together at the design firm. Each day, her mother would express concerns. She didn't like it that I was older than Cheryl, the fact that I'd been married didn't help, and divorced twice, even worse.

Cheryl's father Dan, who'd adopted her when he married her mother, remained neutral. I'd known him for years, having cut his hair back in my Sebring days. He liked me just fine, but he was known to be a hardened businessman who had no time for any sort of nonsense. Once we moved to Woodland Hills, it was too far for me to travel to cut his hair, so I rarely saw him.

As tensions grew between Cheryl and her mother, she resigned from her firm and began to travel with me everywhere. I was being booked on more national TV shows like *What's My Line?*, *To Tell the Truth*, and the *Today Show*.

Cheryl went with me everywhere, even to some of my clients' appointments. The bottom line: I wanted Cheryl by my side. I'd spent my entire life being alone. She'd made tremendous sacrifices to share her life with me, and we were both functioning better as a team.

Takeaways

- The best advice can come from an unexpected source. It's always wise to listen.

- Make room for the important people in your life.

- Growing is not the same as quitting.

- Part of being successful is knowing when to move on.

- Sometimes we all need to change directions.

INGREDIENT #13

WHEN YOU FALL, DON'T PULL OTHERS DOWN WITH YOU

Another sign that my relationship with Paul Newman had gone to another level came in 1978 after he'd won a national racing championship with his Datsun racecar. Paul, who shared my love of fast cars, had started racing professionally in 1972 and often asked me to come with him to the track.

When he decided to move up to open-wheel racing, he offered to sell me his car. The deal included an extra engine, a few sets of tires, and a trailer to haul the racecar. "Listen, Markham, I really think you'd be good at this," he said. "I've already arranged for you to take classes at Skip Barber, he's the guy who taught me. He's the best. It'll be a week in San Francisco."

"How much?" I asked.

"The price for the whole deal—$10,000."

"That's incredibly generous, Paul," I said. "Let me think about it."

After I hung up the phone, I could hardly believe the unique opportunity of driving Paul's car had been offered to me. There would be 13 races in a season over a year.

I wrestled with the decision. I was in the midst of building my business, but I absolutely loved racing and competing. Plus, it was Paul. His offer meant the world to me, but I ran the numbers several times and determined the financial demands of that sport were out of my league.

Vickie decided to return to Farmington once she graduated beauty school, but she and I were now closer than ever. Shortly after she left, Bobby came to live with us in LA to pursue a career in the business.

Life with Cheryl and the reconnection with my children brought me more joy than I'd ever imagined, but the more successful I became with Markham Products, the worse my relationship got with my main partner, Ernie Richardson.

By that time, we'd signed about 75 distributors in 42 states and were operating more than 2,000 certified Markham Innovator shops and salons across the country. 6,000 stylists had earned the Markham certificate, and we'd expanded our two product lines—the Jim Markham $55 Haircut beige line and the Markham for Men black line.

My partner technically only owned 15 percent of the company to my 57 percent; contractually, he maintained equal control until I paid back his investors $50,000 plus 10 percent interest. By the time I realized I'd signed on for a situation where the bar could be moved on me whenever I got close to paying that off, it was too late.

Ernie worked as an attorney, and while he'd been instrumental in launching the company, I'd been the one keeping it operational from the start. My travel schedule had intensified, with a constant stream of educational commitments and client meetings. I'd been pushing hard for more than a dozen years, but I still couldn't afford to let up.

By 1981, we were on track to bring in nearly $2 million in revenue. I was proud that our efforts were proving successful, but Ernie and I were growing more out of sync in our priorities for the company. What had once been a fruitful partnership had soured, and tensions were beginning to grow.

One day, I'd come off the road from a three-week stint only to be met with another round of criticism from Ernie.

Fed up and exhausted, I leaned across his desk until my face was inches from his. "Since you think you know so much more than I do about running Markham, why don't you just buy me out?" My entire body burned with anger.

He smirked and said, "I thought you'd never ask."

After a quick round of tense negotiation, I agreed to sell him 52 percent of my 57 percent for $200,000 with $50,000 as the first down payment. I kept 5 percent.

I knew better, but I was so frustrated with the whole situation that I failed to seek my own legal counsel. In a moment of pure exhaustion and weakness, I allowed myself to break emotionally, and I walked right into his trap.

It was clear that he'd already given this plenty of thought, because he insisted that I sign a highly restrictive, five-year noncompete agreement that meant I couldn't start another hair product company during that time frame. In return, he agreed to pay the lease on my Mercedes-Benz and a $2,500-a-month payment to me over the next five years.

Just like that, in 1981, I no longer owned the company that bore my name. Ernie was large and in charge. And I was left wondering what my future would be.

For the first time since I was 15 years old, I didn't have a job or any place I had to be. With those monthly payments still coming in from Sebring, and more expected from Markham, I had the financial security to get us through the gap.

What gnawed at me was not only that I'd sold Markham Products, but that I'd sold out for nowhere near what the company was worth.

I'd also made a huge mistake by signing a lengthy noncompete clause. Due to that agreement, I was legally prevented from seeking out vendors or working on formulas for five long years! In a moment of impulsiveness fueled by anger, I'd signed away my handsome salary, my glamorous clientele, my membership to the best clubs, and worst of all, my own name and the status it brought me.

With too much time on my hands and just enough money in my pockets, I turned to partying. As an athlete in my younger years and the son of an alcoholic, I rarely drank. I wouldn't even take an aspirin. It wasn't until I got to Hollywood that I'd enjoy an occasional glass of wine.

Cheryl had been even more cautious than me. She was so paranoid about someone slipping her something at a party that she would carry her own food and a diet soda in her purse. Having grown up in Hollywood, she was well aware of the danger—especially for women.

But being back on the party scene brought me back to cocaine—the drug that Jay Sebring had introduced me to in those early days. While I'd experimented occasionally at parties, I'd never dared use it when I was traveling and promoting my business.

By this point, I'd seen enough to know that Jay's old claim about coke being nonaddictive was false. But I had no idea how far nor how fast you could fall into the rabbit hole. I was about to find out, and one of the biggest regrets of my life is that I dragged Cheryl down with me.

Trying to numb our growing anxieties about selling the company and not knowing what to do next, we embarked on a private, nonstop party for two. We isolated ourselves in our beautiful home in Sherman Oaks and disappeared from the Hollywood scene—barely leaving our house at all for months on end.

Soon, we recognized we had a serious problem. We'd enjoyed the high a little too much, and now we couldn't seem to stop. Unfortunately,

The Betty Ford Clinic had not been founded yet, and we couldn't find any sort of facility that provided an effective drug rehab program.

We tried going to Alcoholics Anonymous, but that didn't seem to be the right kind of help for us. The other group members couldn't relate to our kind of addiction, and even the group leaders had trouble understanding our situation. Next, Cheryl called a psychiatrist for guidance, but he insisted he had no experience with cocaine addiction and turned us away.

Every day, we'd make promises to each other about getting clean, but we could not get control of the destructive addiction, no matter how hard we tried.

Spinning out of control financially, I sold the remaining note on the Sebring Products to my old publicist for $50,000 in cash—half its value. The only thing I couldn't cash out was the $2,500 a month that Ernie had agreed to pay over the life of my noncompete and the 5 percent of Markham Products stock I still owned.

As our bank account dwindled, we looked to find something we could do from the confines of our home. Cheryl's Uncle Larry, her mother's older brother, had made a good deal of money with a string of companies. He sold us on an opportunity to use the made-up name Southern Railway Liquidations, which led customers to believe there was a distressed-sales opportunity with merchandise that had "been salvaged from train derailments."

He convinced us that we might be able to make a profit by selling his latest wares: tarps and buck knives. The idea was simple. We would purchase buck knives from him for $3 each and sell them for $9. In return, he would give us his mailing lists, provide warehouse space for the goods, and ship out the orders.

We invested about $7,000 with him. Then we sent out about 25,000 flyers advertising the sale. He'd told us that if even 2 1/2 percent of those target customers responded, then we would make a good return. We diligently sent out those mailings for several months. Finally, it dawned on us—he was running a scam.

I'd always succeeded by working hard, making solid plans, and calculating my every move. But the addiction limited my ability to make good decisions and left me unmotivated to even try. Panic mode settled in.

Cheryl and I were aware that our lives were sinking, fast. We wanted a do-over—some place to start fresh. I concocted this vague plan that I would re-emerge and launch a chain of salons. Cheryl got her courage up and called her parents in hopes they would invest. "Nope, no way," they said. "Not under these circumstances." They hung up.

We quickly ran through the last of our money. Until then, I'd prided myself on paying my bills responsibly. I'd committed to managing my finances well because I'd always hated the times Mom and I were forced to leave in the middle of the night before rent came due. In contrast, Cheryl had experienced a comfortable upbringing, but it had left her unprepared for dealing with the world of debt collectors.

Breaking the news to her proved one of the most difficult things I've ever had to do: "Honey," I swallowed hard. "We don't have enough money to pay our mortgage."

I was terribly afraid. We were out of money and out of options.

The fear of poverty tops the list of the six fears in Napoleon Hill's classic book *Think and Grow Rich*. The author calls it the most destructive of them all. A few of the reasons why fear of poverty tops his list are because it paralyzes your reasoning, kills your imagination, leads to procrastination, destroys ambition, makes it impossible to concentrate, and breeds a whole host of dream killers.

Coming down off coke was beyond brutal, leaving us in the gutter of depression. It had hammered us physically, emotionally, and spiritually. We felt like we'd gone to hell. We were living in a constant state of panic and sleep deprivation. Everything ached—even our bones. The pain was excruciating. One moment we'd be shivering and unable to break the chills; the next minute, we'd be sweating like we were in a sauna. Neither one of us knew how much more we could take. The terrible paranoia left us feeling unsafe and vulnerable, and we were both convinced we were going to die.

I'd been driven by faith in myself and my ability to make big dreams come true for a long time. When I did fail at something, I'd always picked myself up and kept going. But now, for the first time since I was a young teen, I gave in to fear. Actually, we were living in sheer terror.

It was August 1982—13 years since the Manson murders—and yet I was still running from ghosts. It had been about a year since I'd sold Markham, and I began to lose hope.

That's when I made another big mistake. I fell into the trap of chasing my glory days. I decided that Albuquerque would be the best place to launch my comeback. I was sure my old clients would be thrilled about my return.

An old friend offered a spare bedroom and agreed to help me financially. I shared my new plan with Cheryl, telling her that we needed to make an immediate decision since we could no longer pay our bills in LA.

We threw our clothes into our suitcases and loaded up black trash bags with whatever else we could fit into my Mercedes-Benz, including my celebrity photos and scrapbooks. Because we weren't thinking clearly, we left behind virtually all of our possessions worth any monetary value: my extensive album collection, thousands of dollars' worth of electronics and high-end furniture. We dressed stylishly, like two people who didn't have a care in the world, but in reality, we were absolutely destitute. We had no idea what the future held for us.

Neither of us uttered more than a few words on the long drive east. The only sounds were from the radio playing softly. As the lush coastal landscape turned to bone-dry desert, and the glow of the city lights faded in the rearview mirror, I glanced over at Cheryl. She was still wearing her sunglasses, even though the sun had already set behind us. Tears were running down her cheeks.

"You know, Cheryl, we can do this," I said. "This is a new beginning for us."

"I believe you," she said, sitting up and wiping her tears, but she was sad.

"I'm known for comebacks," I said. "Just hold on. This is just a little detour. We're going to get back on the right road. I promise."

I'd made a lot of mistakes at that point, but I was determined to make things right. Cheryl had been the one person who'd stuck with me in life and who had loved me through the ups and downs. If there was one thing I knew to be true, it was that I owed her more than this.

We took I-40 through northern Arizona. When we stopped for lunch, my credit card was refused. I pulled out another and that one had hit the limit, too. Cheryl gave the waitress hers, and it worked. Never had I felt more ashamed.

When we left the restaurant, I gave Cheryl an apologetic look. "We may have to sleep in the car tonight."

Cheryl shook her head no. "From my jobs in retail, I know that after 6:00 p.m. the hotel is unable to check if card is good," she explained. "We just have to get out of the hotel before 6:00 a.m. tomorrow."

We drove as far as Gallup, New Mexico, before stopping for the night. Following Cheryl's plan, we checked in after dark and got up before the sun rose, leaving an easy drive into Albuquerque for the next day.

I felt bad about skipping out on our bill, but my back was up against the wall. As always, Cheryl had a plan for that, too. "Babe, listen," she said. "I've got this little notebook. I'm keeping record of what we owe to whom. The date, the amount. Everything. That way as soon as we get back on our feet, we can make it right." (Little did we know that American Express and Visa also kept record. It would take us a number of years to pay back all that we owed plus 25 percent in penalties and interest.)

By the time we arrived in Albuquerque at my friend's house in the northeast foothills, he and his wife welcomed us warmly.

They'd just sat down for dinner, but quickly pulled up two extra chairs and made us feel right at home.

The next day, my friend and I discussed my plans for a new shop called Markham. After encouraging me through each idea, he grew serious and said, "I figure in return for my investment, I should own a third of your business."

I was stunned. I sat there for a minute staring at his stern face. *That's all I need,* I thought. *Another partner who knows nothing about the hair business taking such a large cut while I do all the work.*

"Are you serious?" I asked, determined not to repeat past mistakes no matter how desperate I'd become.

"I'm dead serious. Do we have a deal or not?"

"I can't give up a third of my income for that small of an investment," I reasoned.

"Well, from where I sit, you don't have much of a choice."

I exhaled. He was right. But no matter how little bargaining power I had at the time, I wasn't willing to sign another bad deal. I mustered all my strength and said, "I'm sorry, but no thanks."

Takeaways

- Think long and hard before partnering with someone.

- A successful partnership requires mutual respect and a willingness to entertain new ideas.

- Never make a life-altering decision in an emotionally charged moment.

- Always maintain the controlling interest in a company.

- Be leery of a long noncompete.

- Pay your debts.

- Never lose yourself to addiction.

- Don't hurt the people who love and trust you.

- Recognize when a potential partner is offering a bad deal. Walk away no matter how desperate you are.

INGREDIENT #14

IT HELPS TO HAVE FAITH

Once the sun came up, Cheryl and I bid the couple farewell and drove over to see my long-time friends Frank and Sandra Stockton. They owned a successful Markham Style Innovator shop called Stockton's Hair Artists and had established themselves as successful Markham distributors for New Mexico and Colorado. The Christian couple were extremely talented stylists and had been distributors for Sebring as well. Frank had worked with me at many hair shows.

I explained a little about our situation, and before I could finish, Frank interrupted and said, "Stay here with us. We've got five kids and just three bedrooms, so there's not a lot of space, but you're more than welcome to stay as long as you need."

Frank's warm welcome eased my anxieties enough to share my plan to start Markham's Celebrity Cuts with the bigger dream of turning it into a chain of salons.

The Stocktons offered encouragement, but they both knew we were detoxing from the drugs. But instead of turning us away, they supported us. They made us feel like family and prayed for us. They made us feel safe at a time when we needed it most.

That first Sunday morning, we all piled into their VW van and went with them to church. It was a big congregation in the valley. Even though I'd been part of the Mormon church for a few years during my first marriage, I was completely unfamiliar with the born-again movement that Frank and Sandra were a part of. To Cheryl, who is Jewish, the religion was completely foreign. The congregation actively spoke in tongues and laid hands on those who were struggling with various illnesses and ailments. The Stocktons got the entire congregation to pray for us. For the first time in our lives, we felt surrounded by unconditional love.

Soon, we were going on prayer walks in the desert with the Stocktons and their friends Larry and Sandra. With patient guidance, these two couples shepherded us toward salvation. Before long, Cheryl and I were attending church serves regularly on Sundays and Wednesdays. We found the messages about love and forgiveness encouraging.

Gradually, the intense pain and brain fog of withdrawals eased for both of us. I began searching for a shop to rent, hoping to build a salon that would appeal to both men and women. I'd learned from Markham Products that there was much more potential with female clientele.

The first month went by and no check came from my former partner. When I called to make sure he had my new address, he told me his accountant had found some old liabilities on the books that were personally my responsibility.

"You can't be serious," I said.

"Oh, yes, I am," said Ernie. "I won't be sending your $2,500 this month or next."

"But I've got bills to pay, and I was counting on that money," I argued. I could feel the old fight well up in my chest. *He's lucky he's almost 800 miles away.* "You should know, I plan to call my new salon Markham. I assume you have no issue with that," I said.

"You bet I have a problem with that," he roared.

My throat pulsed with intensity.

"There's nothing you can do about it, Jim," he continued, shouting through the phone. "I bought the exclusive rights to your name. I saw what you did with Sebring. You waltzed out of there and took all the best ideas and implemented them under your own name. It's called a noncompete for a reason. You must think I'm a moron."

"So you're telling me I can't use my own name? For my own salon?" I felt incredulous. "I've got to be able to make a living, Ernie. And cutting hair is the only thing I know how to do. I thought the noncompete was just to preclude me from having my own product line."

"Well, I guess you should have paid more attention to what you were signing. I own the Markham name whether it's on a bottle, a shop, or a T-shirt. If I hear about you using the Markham name, you won't see another penny from me. Our deal will be null and void. Got it?"

I slowly hung up the phone, stunned by the venom in his voice.

We had been in New Mexico for almost two months. I had no money coming in, no place to call our own, and now I felt like a man who'd been robbed of the one thing I had left—my name.

Over the past 13 years, I had learned that branding a name was critically important. I'd poured so much into Sebring and then Markham. This latest blow knocked me back hard.

"Cheryl, maybe you should think about going back to Los Angeles and asking your mom for your old job back," I said. For the first time, I was doubtful I could make things work, and I didn't want to risk dragging her down with me any further.

"No way, Jim," she said. "I told you I'm not going anywhere. That's what you do when you love somebody—you stick with them in good times and bad. We'll get through this, baby. I believe in you. You know why?"

I couldn't imagine a single reason. "Why?" I said.

"Because *you* are my Jim Markham."

Just when I'd run out of options, Bobby Lewis, one of my top distributors with Markham, reached out to me unexpectedly from his home in Oklahoma. "I heard you're living in Albuquerque and that you've become Christians," he said.

"Yes, Cheryl and I made big changes in our lives," I explained. "We're living with the Stocktons until we get back on our feet. They've taught us a lot."

He seemed pleased with the positive updates and asked about our future plans. "You think you'll open a new shop out there?"

"Well, I definitely want to start my own place once again," I admitted. "I have faith that something will work out in time."

He didn't hesitate before asking, "How much do you think you're going to need to get started?"

"I've thought a lot about that. I'm certain I could do it with $25,000."

"That's the exact number I thought you'd give," Bobby said. "Well, Pam and I have prayed about it, and we want to loan you that money. My only question is: What do you have for collateral?"

I was quiet for a moment, surprised by his offer. "I can give you my remaining 5 percent of Markham Products stock."

"That sounds fine," he said. "It's settled then. Why don't you and Cheryl come visit Pam and me this weekend? We'll work out all the details and get you back on your feet."

I was never so grateful, and I certainly never saw this coming.

When Cheryl and I arrived by Friday evening, Bobby and Pam welcomed us with open arms, treating us like family. "Let's get this out of the way," Bobby said, pulling the check out from his shirt pocket. "I figured you could relax and enjoy our time together if you had it in your hands."

I was so accustomed to people playing games, his openness and trust caught me off guard. We talked late into the night about our faith, our new Christian lifestyle, and my plans for the salon. I told him what Cheryl and I had discussed about Celebrity Cuts, the possibility of opening a franchised chain and the problem I'd run into over my name with my former partner.

"Sounds like a raw deal, Jim," he said. "But sometimes what appears to be a curse winds up producing our greatest blessings. God led you to where you need to be. We become greater when we are willing to learn the lessons God is working to teach us."

On Sunday, we accompanied the couple to services at the Church of Christ. I'd never been to a Church of Christ service. All I knew was that my mom's parents had been members.

After dinner Sunday night, Bobby said, "Now I've got an important question for you, Jim. Do you plan to marry Cheryl? She seems like an awfully good woman."

"Well, we've talked about it several times, but we wanted to wait until we could get my kids together and have her family with us," I said. "She's never been married before, and we wanted to do it right. But the logistics of trying to get that many people together in one place is difficult.

"Why don't you just do it right here after Wednesday night's service?" Bobby asked. "I could check with the preacher, and I'm sure we could put on a beautiful ceremony for you."

Cheryl and I looked at each other and laughed in response to the surprising suggestion. But laughter quickly turned to genuine smiles. With nothing but love in my heart, I took her hand and said, "Let's do it, Cheryl."

First thing Monday morning, we went to City Hall to get our marriage license. Then we bought matching gold bands for $35 each.

We married on October 20, 1982, in Oklahoma City. With short notice, we had no time to invite any family. Bobby Lewis stood up for me as best man, and his wife Pam lent her wedding dress to Cheryl. Their daughter served as flower girl, and their son stood as ringbearer and the preacher performed the ceremony with the small congregation as witnesses.

In front of the altar, Cheryl proudly took my name as her own.

By the time we were on our way back to Albuquerque, I had a check for $25,000 in my wallet—the seed money for Celebrity Cuts—and my new bride by my side.

Takeaways

- Miracles can come from unexpected sources.

- When we believe in ourselves, it inspires others to have faith in us too.

- God has a plan in the works, even when we can't yet see what's up ahead.

- Unconditional love is a powerful thing.

- It's okay to accept help when it's offered to us.

- We can't identify unhealthy behaviors until we have a firm understanding of what's healthy.

INGREDIENT #15

GRATITUDE IS KEY

I was eager to get back to business, and I was elated to finally have some money again. After more than a year of functioning in survival mode, I finally felt free again to dream, plan, and strategize. The delay on being able to open my new salon had given me plenty of time to refamiliarize myself with Albuquerque and select a site—a small place in a strip mall next to a busy gas station on Menaul Boulevard, located in Albuquerque's Northeast Heights. We thought the site would be perfect. Ironically, it was also near the location of my old Sebring International Shop. Life had come full circle.

Our next priority was to find our own housing. We found a fourth-floor, furnished, two-bedroom apartment within two miles of the salon. The rent was reasonable, and the complex had four washing machines and two dryers on each floor—a perk that would prove ideal for washing the towels from the salon, since we could no longer afford a laundry service.

Ever optimistic, Cheryl didn't complain. Instead, she said, "Well, at least we have an elevator, so we won't have to lug everything up the steps."

Thanksgiving was just around the corner, and we had so much to be grateful for. With the help and support of our new church family and the power of God, we had both kicked the drugs and found deep faith. The church had served as our rehab before there was such a thing. The people there had delivered us from the hell of addiction and saved our lives.

It's no exaggeration to say we'd truly been born again. We found a fresh new start in the industry that meant so much to me and a supportive community to embrace our efforts. But more than that, I'd married a beautiful, kind-hearted woman I loved, a true partner who had proven in countless ways that she loved me *for richer or poorer, in sickness and in health*. And we finally had a place to call home again.

There was only one problem. Once again, my former partner in Markham failed to send the payment that month. I'd been dealing with bullies since childhood, and I'd learned the hard way how people like that would continue to target me until I stood up for myself. This time I didn't pull any punches. I called Ernie and demanded my money. "I have two attorneys who said they'd be happy to help me," I said. "Start paying what you promised. No more games."

I had no real intentions of suing Ernie, and I certainly wasn't in a position to back up my threat, but it had the desired effect. A check came in the mail the following week along with a curt note reminding me that the lease on my Mercedes was expiring in January, and I would need to turn it in to the dealer in Hollywood. Despite his best attempts to rattle me, I elected to stay focused on my new venture and leave the rest in the past.

If you'd asked me how I felt about the situation with Ernie, I'd have sworn I'd let it go. But sometimes the body holds stress in ways we don't even realize. Life was about to teach me another valuable lesson, this one about the body, mind, and spirit connection.

Just as I was opening our new shop, I developed a cough deep in my chest. Next came a fever, and my lungs began to burn in pain. That night, I woke up coughing with a fever, and I was shaking badly. A visit to the emergency room revealed that I had pneumonia.

Day after day, my condition worsened. Aside from withdrawals, I'd never been this sick in my entire life.

The doctors were struggling to get my lungs clear and had prescribed several different antibiotics without any relief. More than once, I suggested Cheryl return to LA and stay with her parents. It pained me to see her taking care of me. We were just getting back on our feet, and here I was again, feeling like a burden. It sunk me.

With her extensive design background, Cheryl landed a job with American Furniture—a firm known for high-end design. The first three months, she was given a small salary, but then moved to full commission. Despite some challenges, she worked very hard every day and managed to create her own clients in record time. Her regular paycheck during my recovery helped keep us from draining our start-up funds, and I was grateful to have such a strong partner.

Most days I was alone with my thoughts while Cheryl was at work. I spent my time praying and thinking about my life. When I reached my lowest lows, I relied on my newfound faith to sustain me.

What are you trying to teach me, God? Humility? Trust? What is it that you think I still need to learn? I think I'm ready now. Please let me get well.

During the Christmas season, I forced myself to think about all the miracles that had happened over the last few months. I thanked God for allowing us to survive going cold turkey from such an addictive drug.

I thought about the miracle of Frank and Sandra taking us in, no questions asked, despite five children and a million reasons to turn us away. I thought about Bobby Lewis who'd invested $25,000, giving me the opportunity for a new business.

And I thought about Cheryl—a life partner I could truly count on. Someone who loved me through the ups and downs, without question.

I thought about the lifelong friends, people who were there for me, standing by me through the lowest points of my journey.

I saw it all as miracles.

Although I'd had solid employees with both Sebring and Markham, I'd largely relied on my workhorse habits to pull the companies through the rough patches. The many betrayals I'd experienced both personally and professionally had made it hard for me to trust. Plus, let's face it, I'd made a ton of mistakes on my own. Now I was building my circle of trust—people I could count on and who could count on me. It was time for me to let go of the wheel.

Finally, I surrendered. With my mind no longer racing, I drifted off into a long, peaceful rest. I released my need for control and put my faith in God.

Just after the New Year in 1983, my health finally returned.

One of the first Sunday mornings I felt well enough to attend church, a speaker was visiting from Dallas. He spoke to the congregation of about 300 people—mostly blue collar and Hispanic. At the end of his sermon, he asked people to come forward and accept Jesus as their savior. Suddenly, he pointed straight at me and said, "You are going to be world famous someday."

A jolt of energy blew through me. As crazy as his words sounded at that moment, I'd seen my share of miracles by then, and I was a believer.

With my health finally restored, we forged ahead and opened Celebrity Cuts by Jim Markham, the prototype for the chain we planned to eventually spread across the country. Before I gave up my Mercedes, I drove to Lubbock with my brother Bobby, who had earned an auto dealer's license by that time. He took me to an auction where I bid $500 for an old Datsun pickup with a lot of miles on it. I won the bid, paid cash, and drove it home. It wasn't a smoking hot Mercedes by any stretch of the imagination. In fact, the only thing smoking about my pickup was that it burned oil. But it was practical and would suffice for the back-and-forth trips to the salon.

By then, I'd learned some big lessons about money management, and was proceeding cautiously with the limited funding we'd been given. Gone were the high-living, big-spending days I'd known. Now, we made an artform of frugality. Growing up poor, I had been financially illiterate. I'd found early success with my first two businesses, but I had absolutely no understanding of how to manage my money. I appreciated the fresh start and knew all too well how quickly we could lose it all again if we weren't careful.

To save money, Cheryl and I built out the 650-square-foot salon ourselves. Our buddies Frank and Larry pitched in with their wives, bringing meals, helping Cheryl bargain hunt for furnishings. They became family to us.

We installed a new black-and-white linoleum floor and attached mirrors throughout the shop. My collection of autographed celebrity photos hung on the walls.

Cheryl bargain hunted at thrift shops, outfitting the salon to appeal to both sexes—especially women. She found four chairs at a junkyard and ordered burnt orange colored vinyl fabric to re-cover them. It was a great look against the black-and-white backdrop. By the time Cheryl worked her magic, the unisex salon had a sleek, modern feel, despite our limited budget.

The salon was coming along nicely, and I'd just begun to exhale when I got another shock. I called my ex-partner to order Markham Products to retail to my clients. Much to my surprise, Ernie flatly refused to give them to me at the distributor's price.

Again, my old Markham distributor friend (and investor) Bobby Lewis came to my aid: "Don't worry, Jim," he said. "I'll sell you the products at the distributor's price. After all you've done for my business, that's the least I can do."

On the women's side, I decided to use Paul Mitchell products. I also stocked Redken because I wanted to carry at least three lines.

I spent some of our precious startup capital by hiring a PR person. I got a decent amount of press, but hardly anyone showed up for the grand opening. Standing there with just a handful of friends at the ribbon cutting, I became painfully aware of how quickly you can be forgotten. I worried about what I'd gotten us into. *Could we climb out of this hole?*

The next few months proved especially slow, for both the stylists I'd hired and for me. I had plenty of time to think about what was going wrong. Let me start by saying the data showed that $10 to $15 was the average going rate for haircuts in Albuquerque in 1983. I'd already dropped my price from the $75 I'd most recently charged in Hollywood to $35 for a cut, style, and blow-dry at the new salon. But that price was still too expensive in the New Mexico market—especially in a town filled with other stylists I trained in my technique who were offering the "$55 Haircut for a whole lot less."

I'd drive past other salons with my name above the door and see the cars packed in the parking lot. I felt so foolish for selling the rights to my own name. In effect, I had priced myself out of the market I was competing in, all while being blocked from using the well-known Markham name in my own town.

It turned out that old clients hadn't been sitting around breathlessly waiting for my return to Albuquerque. In truth, I was viewed as outrageously expensive—especially by the men.

The other hard truth was that my skills as a stylist were rusty. For the last dozen years, I'd primarily focused on running the companies and had spent little time behind the chair. I also lacked the experience with women's hair, in comparison to my expertise with men's styling.

I eventually lowered my price to $25. As much as this bothered me, it proved to be the magic number. I finally booked up and added three more stylists. I was determined to make it work.

I was in the salon by 8:30 every morning and didn't usually turn out the lights until 6:00 p.m. As business grew, I extended the hours from 7:00 a.m. to 7:00 p.m. Eventually, the salon was booming with five stylists, including myself and a manicurist.

Cheryl was moving up in her career, too. She was named the top in-store salesperson/designer almost every month at American Furniture.

Eventually, we saved enough money to buy a second car—a used VW Bug—which enabled Cheryl to have more flexibility to go to customers' homes to consult.

Despite our long workdays, every night Cheryl and I washed loads of towels for the salon the next morning. That was a far cry from how she'd grown up in Hollywood with a full-time housekeeper, but she never complained.

That spring, my old friend Wolfman Jack came through town with his daughter. They were traveling from California to Virginia and stopped to spend the night with us. Of course, I was thrilled to see my friend, and I offered to cut his hair while he was checking out the new shop. While he was in my chair, I said, "Thanks for calling, Wolfman. A lot of people have forgotten about me."

"Jim, you're one of the few people who never asked anything of me," he said. "You're just my friend, a true friend, and that's a rare thing." Then he added, "Speaking of rare things, I want you to know I'm proud of you, man. You're my hero. Look, if you hadn't run out of money, we would have been praying over you like John Belushi. You're the only cat I've ever seen come back from all that."

I fought my emotions, knowing he was right. "I'm very lucky to be alive, Wolfman. And for that, I'm truly grateful."

Takeaways

- As soon as you hit a dead end, turn around and find the path you should be on.

- Stand up to bullies—especially in business.

- Remain focused on your strengths.

- Find the good and practice gratitude daily.

- Look for the lessons.

- You can make a comeback. And another. And another.

INGREDIENT #16

IT'S NEVER TOO LATE TO CHOOSE LOVE

Cheryl and I made a complete change in our lifestyle. God had answered our prayers. By this time, we were attending church services twice a week and were completely free of addiction. We were focused on rebuilding our careers, and any spare time on our hands was spent taking advantage of Albuquerque's beautiful outdoor activities. Together, we rode bikes, hiked mountain trails, and enjoyed aerobics classes at a local gym where I also learned to play racquetball. In addition, I frequently ran laps around the local high school track. We were both in the best shape of our lives, and it felt good to reclaim our health, especially after the long, hard phase of withdrawals followed by my intense battle back from pneumonia.

It had been three years since we'd seen Cheryl's parents. The relationship with her family had been strained since Cheryl had moved in with me back in Los Angeles, but once the business fell apart and the drugs took over, everything quickly unraveled. Every time I suggested that Cheryl go visit her family, she refused. Wounds remained unhealed and it felt easier to just stay busy and focus on rebuilding our lives. But Cheryl's mother, Arline, reached out one day to discover that we'd not only gotten clean and married, but that we were both happy and healthy in Albuquerque. She immediately booked a flight to New Mexico to check up on us. Once she saw that we truly were genuinely doing well, she cheerfully announced: "We need to celebrate. I'm taking you both shopping."

It seemed life was delivering miracles at every turn, and yet starting over was proving to be a lot harder than I'd ever imagined. I'd been working in the industry since I was 15 years old. I'd started from nothing and had worked my way all the way to the top—not once, but twice. But in Albuquerque, none of that meant much. In fact, it might have even been a hindrance, because people would routinely walk into the shop and ask, "Why are you here? Shouldn't you be in Hollywood?"

I was stumped about how to answer that question. The last thing I wanted was to explain all the mistakes that had brought us back to New Mexico. Cheryl's mother came up with the perfect answer. "Tell them you love the people here," Arline said. "That's why you came back."

Arline was smart, but she was also right. The truth was, we had fallen in love with the people of Albuquerque, and they seemed satisfied with that answer.

On the surface, I was just another guy trying to earn a living. But my mind was still working on overdrive—planning and strategizing a full comeback. I was determined to make Celebrity Cuts successful as a national franchise.

Three years after returning to Albuquerque, I called my ex-wife Lena. It wasn't the first time I'd reached out since she'd removed Jay from my life. Each Christmas and on his birthday, I'd been sending him a check and gifts, hoping Lena would let him have them or at the least put the money in an account for him. But every time, my letters and gifts were returned unopened.

I'd regularly started trying to get in touch with Jay once he turned 12. Lena had promised me she'd sit him down at some point and let him know the truth about his name. But as far as I knew, he was still being raised as Jay Clark, even though he was never formally adopted by his stepfather. And every time I traveled near west Texas, I called for him, hoping to visit. Lena always put me off.

Now, shortly after Jay's sixteenth birthday in March 1984, yet another package came back unopened. Cheryl encouraged me to try and give him a call.

With her support, I reached out and asked for Jay. I also had a question for Lena. "Why didn't you at least deposit the checks I've sent him? He would have had a nice nest egg by now."

Lena avoided any kind of conflict. "It's complicated, Jim. I have another son to think about. How could I explain why his brother got all these gifts and money that he didn't get?" The rise in her pitch was the only indication that she was upset. Her husband worked in the oilfields, so I suspected things were tight.

"Did you tell him yet?"

She stuttered through a few excuses and promised to tell him soon.

"Do it, Lena. Please," I insisted. "We had a deal."

I called back a few days later and asked to speak to my son.

"He's really confused and upset about finding out that his real name is Markham and not Clark," she said. "He's got a lot of questions."

"I'm sure he does," I said, "Will you please ask him to come to the phone?"

After a brief pause, she came back on the line. "He's not ready yet, Jim. I think he's scared to talk to you."

Frustrated, I said goodbye and hung up.

Two weeks later, I got a call from Lena. "Jay is ready now," she said. Then she put my son on the line.

"Hi, Dad," he said in the soft Texas accent that I knew so well. Tears came to my eyes. I'd never heard him speak. He had lived almost his entire life in the tiny town of Snyder, between Lubbock and Abilene.

He'd been so close to me, and yet so far, these last few years, and he hadn't even known I'd existed. I had been tempted so many times to march to their door and demand to see him, but I respectfully honored Lena's wishes, as I promised to do.

Now, after all this time, I was being granted a new beginning. Before we hung up, I invited him to come for a week's visit as soon as school was out. "I'll send you an airline ticket," I said.

"That sounds great. Thanks, Dad."

When he arrived at the airport, I recognized Jay instantly. My son looked a lot like me and carried himself in the exact same way. As soon as he saw me, he broke into a grin and gave me a big hug.

His first request was to get a haircut, so we drove straight to the salon where I treated him like a VIP. He stared at the celebrities on the wall for a long time before turning to me with his eyes glistening. Through tears he said, "I'm glad you're my dad."

I put my hand on his shoulder and said, "I waited a very long time for this moment, son."

Just as she'd done with Vickie and Bobby, Cheryl welcomed Jay warmly. We could both see immediately that he had been sheltered, but over the course of the week, we also got small clues into how rough Jay's life had been. He loved baseball but couldn't participate because he couldn't afford the glove and the uniform. A baseball glove, a bat, and all the gear he would have needed was in one of the many packages I'd sent him over the years—the packages that always came back marked *return to sender.*

He seemed close to his younger half-brother, which made me happy. Jay's stepfather was tall, with dark hair and eyes. In contrast, Jay was small for his age and blonde with blue eyes. Jay admitted he'd always wondered if his stepdad was his real father. He was echoing the same thoughts I had as a kid—wondering if my dad was my real dad.

He told me that his stepdad drank a lot. "He's a good guy when he's not drinking," he said.

I had plenty of questions of my own at that point, but I was still feeling my way into my son's life and was afraid to push too hard too fast. I hadn't much practice being a father, and the only thing I knew to offer him at this point was my unconditional love.

Before the end of the week, I gave him a copy of Dale Carnegie's *How to Win Friends and Influence People*. "This is one of the books that changed my life when I was about your age," I said. "Call me after you read it and we'll talk about it." Then I gave him a hug and added, "You can make your life anything you want it to be, son. I'm going to help you figure out how."

When it was time for Jay to return to Texas, I watched teary-eyed as he walked to the gate at the airport, and I wondered when I might see him again. The thought of sending him back to his stepfather, who drank, was painful for me. But I knew as well as anyone that a boy needed his mother, too.

Takeaways

- Mend fences.

- Focus forward.

- When someone offers you love, receive it, and give even more to them in return.

- Family matters.

LEARN FROM THE BEST

L ife was good. With family relationships restored and both of our careers on track. We were very busy, but we used our rare off hours to investigate the franchise chains popping up across the country. Command Performance, Fantastic Sams and Supercuts had all begun franchising in the late 1970s. Nobody seemed to be making a lot of money, and the clientele seemed to care more about the cut being quick and cheap.

This approach didn't fit my business strategy at all. My entire career had been quality and being best in class. Turning Celebrity Cuts into a chain would require a lot of startup capital. I had no doubt I could raise the money if I set my mind to it. The problem was that my heart wasn't in it. In fact, it drained my energy just thinking about it.

It was time for me to move on, just as Cheryl had done earlier in her own career.

Once I acknowledged that launching a franchise wasn't for me, I was free again to explore new ideas. That's when Cheryl asked, "What makes you most excited about the hair care industry? And what do you have to offer that's unique to anyone else out there?"

As soon as I began to think about my true passion and natural talents, the answer became clear: "I want to get back into the product business," I said. The realization was a turning point for me. Shifting back to developing innovative products such as shampoos and conditioners suddenly rekindled a fire in me.

Twice I flew to Toronto for a week's worth of classes with Martin Parsons, a well-known platform artist and member of Intercoiffure — the most powerful and influential organization in the hair industry. I also went to San Francisco twice to attend Vidal Sassoon's Academy for women's hair cutting. I wanted to get more advanced in styling women, and Martin Parsons and Vidal Sassoon were both undisputed leaders in that field.

About the same time, I traveled to Denver to see Horst Rechelbacher, the founder of Aveda Products. Horst had quickly become known for his groundbreaking aromatherapy-based products. The Austrian had launched his first hair care products in 1978. Like me, he'd begun working in the industry as a young teen, winning multiple awards for his talent at styling.

I was permitted to go backstage and watch him do a complete makeover on an African-American model. He straightened, cut, colored, highlighted, and dressed out her hair. Then he expertly applied her makeup and photographed the result. Next, he took a Caucasian model through the same makeover process—except for the step of straightening her hair. It was remarkable to see someone so talented in all those different areas and equally as good with such diverse models. Horst could do it all. I had never seen anything like it. I studied his teachings on a deep level.

By the time Paul Mitchell Systems launched in Beverly Hills in 1980, it was the hottest thing out there. Paul, an entertaining and gifted Scotsman, had become known for a new technique called "hair sculpting." When I saw that he was coming to Albuquerque, I bought a ticket to his show, eager to see this artist who was generating so much buzz.

Funny and positive, Paul skillfully used his product to sculpt the hair in place to the desired look. Then he put a hooded dryer over the head. The Scotsman, sometimes donning a kilt, would call out to the crowd while demonstrating his unique technique. "Let the hair dryer do the work. Don't be a human water extractor." Then he'd brush it out and spray it with sculpting hairspray to the style he wanted.

I was so impressed by his performance that I went to see him again in San Francisco. In addition to admiring his stage presence and talents behind the chair, I embraced his strong stance against animal testing.

Paul Mitchell wasn't the only one revolutionizing the market with professional hair care products. A renaissance was underway with many stylists launching their own lines. I devoted myself to observing and surveying the best of the best. I loved watching Geri Cuzenza at the big hair shows. She worked five chairs at once, teaching the entire time she was styling. She and her husband John Sebastian had co-founded John Sebastian International, Inc.—a hair care product and beauty company. Another star on the scene was Jeanne Bra, who frequently joined Paul Mitchell on stage before earning her own spotlight. All of these leaders had something to teach me, and I soaked up every skill I could learn.

I also began to think of my temporary lockout from the products business as a blessing in disguise. I was confident that the time I was bringing myself up to speed and studying my competitors would pay off in spades.

My new goal became clear: By the time I'd make my comeback, I'd be the hippest, most cutting-edge entrepreneur in the women's hair care products business, bringing the highest-performing and most innovative products and hair-cutting techniques directly to my customers. I was on a mission and I would not quit until I'd made my dreams come true.

What we needed was a business plan to entice investors to bet on the new hair care product company I'd envisioned. The problem was that neither Cheryl nor I knew what should be in an extensive business plan targeted to investors.

By that point in my career, I'd run two well-known product companies. I easily could have let my pride stop me from asking for help. But what I'd learned is that nobody is smart enough to be an expert in everything. Nobody.

I'd heard about an economic development program through New Mexico State University. It had been geared for those who had a small business idea that could bring jobs to the state. For the next two years, we worked on the business plan with a woman assigned to us named Marsha Bartlett. She held her master's degree in business. My idea was to create a line of high-performance products for women that would offer a more natural alternative to the harsh chemicals being used in many of the hair care products at that time. We called it Genis Pure and Natural, choosing Cheryl's maiden name since my noncompete meant we couldn't use mine.

However, after three years of shopping for an investor, we'd come up empty handed.

We were told the potential investors had a hard time envisioning a stylist as a businessperson. Most stylists who came out with a product line simply hired a lab and slapped his or her name on the label. My approach was the opposite. I wanted to be involved in every aspect of the business. I found the entire process around product development fascinating and could hardly wait to get back in the game.

With no luck finding investors, we finally turned to Cheryl's father. We sent our 70-page business plan to him. He was very successful with his own companies, Modern Video Film and New Wave, which both provided opticals, titles, and post-production services for the film industry. He specialized in explosions and mixing animation with live action, and in addition to his Oscar nomination for *Cabaret*, he'd gained special recognition for creating the famous light saber and other Oscar-winning special effects for *Star Wars*.

From Dan's standpoint, betting on me was a big risk. He had known me since my days at Sebring and seen my success with both my hair companies, but he'd also witnessed me crash and burn and drag Cheryl down with me.

Before he'd even entertain our proposal, I'd have to earn back his trust.

Cheryl and I flew to LA to meet with Dan and Arline at their Hollywood Hills home on Mulholland Drive. A copy of the business plan marked with red ink was spread across the kitchen table, indicating he'd taken time to analyze it carefully.

Dan got straight down to the business at hand. "Here are my conditions," he said. "You've got to have a partner, another well-known stylist who is an expert at women's hair."

Given my track record, the idea of bringing in a partner disturbed me, but when I hesitated to answer, Dan remained firm.

"That happens or no deal," he said, as if he'd read my mind. "Secondly, I want to be involved in all contract negotiations. I think that's an area where I can help you a lot."

I nodded. He was right about my limited understanding of contract negotiations, and I was grateful for his advice.

"Third," he eyed his wife and then me. "You've got to come back to Los Angeles."

"No problem," I said. I'd missed the faster pace and celebrity circles I'd once enjoyed. But that wasn't the only reason Los Angeles appealed to me. I knew Cheryl needed to be near her family. We'd spent too much time estranged, and this would be a chance to heal old wounds.

As Dan laid out the details, he explained that if I accepted this take-it-or-leave-it deal, I would only own one-third of my new company. I'd also carry a $150,000 loan at 11 percent interest—a steep rate. I knew $150,000 wasn't enough money to start a products company, but it would help significantly when combined with the $105,000 that Cheryl and I had managed to save.

My head swam through the previous bad deals I'd signed in the industry. With Sebring, I'd owned a third of the company. With Markham, I'd owned 57 percent and had to pay back a $50,000 loan. Once again, it became clear that I was going to do all the work and yet I was giving away two-thirds of the company right from the start.

Maybe I was foolish. Maybe I was courageous. Or maybe I was just simply out of options. So I stood and I shook my father-in-law's hand, saying simply, "Dan, you've got a deal."

Takeaways

- Think of a problem as an opportunity to find a better way.

- We all have certain gifts and things that we are good at. Follow your passion.

- Invest in learning. If you aren't continually learning what's new, you'll be left behind.

- Don't let what you don't know hold you back. If you really want to learn, you can.

- No one person has all the answers. Ask for help when you need it.

- Find successful mentors to guide you in different areas of your life.

INGREDIENT #18

FOLLOW YOUR OWN INSTINCTS

After being shut out from the product development business for close to a decade, I was thrilled to be given a chance to get back to what I loved. For me there's never been anything better than being in the lab and coming up with a terrific new formula — especially if it opens up a whole new level of hair care for consumers.

But with our latest startup, we were facing some big challenges. Mainly, we were undercapitalized. To solve this problem, Dan required that we find a partner. After a careful search, we found someone who presented the background as both an educator and a platform artist, having taught many classes for Paul Mitchell Systems. Alan Bush, a tall, gangly charismatic Brit, owned an academy called ABBA in Cerritos, California. Although I wasn't thrilled with the idea of taking on an equal partner, he did fit the bill.

We officially started the company in 1988, and after discussing our strengths and interests, we agreed that Alan would handle most educational events and shows while I would handle the product formulation and manage the business. I liked the name of his academy and so did Dan, so we changed our company name from Genis to ABBA. Of course, Alan was gung-ho about the idea, but he didn't want to use the words "Pure and Natural" in the name, replacing them with "Liquid Styling Tools."

"It worked well for Paul Mitchell," he insisted.

"True, but I'm not so sure that means it's going to work for us," I replied, reluctant to let go of the Pure and Natural branding, and hesitant to latch onto the tails of another brand. I wasn't sure how Paul's partner would feel about the idea. When Alan stood firm on the matter, I said, "Let me call John Paul DeJoria and see if he has a problem with it."

To my surprise, JP—as he's known—gave us the green light, allowing us to use the Paul Mitchell tagline in our product's name. Genis Pure and Natural became ABBA Liquid Styling Tools.

As the business developed, Alan offered current market insight that proved valuable, but he stayed out of the day-to-day operations. Dan and I communicated via frequent telephone calls as he helped me through the details of entrepreneurship. Just as I had done when Jay Sebring was my mentor, I called Dan frequently to seek his advice.

As soon as the seed money had been secured, we started working on formulas. Those three and a half years I'd spent scouring trade magazines, asking questions, and studying other products had allowed me to develop strong ideas about natural ingredients. This enabled me to work hand-in-hand with the chemists to produce the results I wanted. I also knew which essences would lead to a nice fragrance, but having a product that smelled great wasn't enough. The product also had to do the job it promised to do.

To save money, Alan, Dan, and I agreed that we should go with stock bottles and stock caps. We didn't have the time, nor the budget required for custom options. The designer presented six designs for our new logo, and we all agreed on a simple series of geometric shapes. The new logo matched the gray lettering.

When we introduced the new line, we came out of the gate with only four products: CremeMoist Shampoo, MoistureScentsation Conditioner, GelLotion, and Exacting Spray. Alan and I were featured in the marketing and advertising spots. While our budget limited us to black-and-white print ads, we aimed to make a strong impact by presenting photos that looked dark and somewhat dramatic, especially with Alan's long, black hair in contrast to my lighter tones.

We shipped our first products late in 1989. Because I'd been out of product development for so long, I needed to find all new vendors for ABBA. Dan helped me become a better negotiator and emphasized the importance of getting multiple quotes. "You don't necessarily want to take the lowest bidder," he explained. "But knowing what the low bid is gives you leverage with the vendor you think will do the best job."

As a small business owner, I hadn't always taken the time to thoroughly check out our vendors. For that same reason, many entrepreneurs only get one bid, accept it, and then they move on. But Dan taught me to take my time before making an important decision like that. That simple strategy saved us from many costly mistakes in the long run.

Before I committed to a corporate attorney, CPA or insurance agent, I interviewed candidates who fit our profile and who understood our scope and vision for ABBA. I learned the importance of finding professionals who had a firm grasp of our particular business, and I refused to settle for any who weren't a perfect fit.

Getting our distribution right for ABBA required a lot of thought, too. By the time I'd finally made my comeback, I was dealing with a very different target market—one that included tons of competitors and a wiser, more mature female shopper. Distribution strategies would need to be completely different from those I'd utilized in the men's market.

The best way to reach the high-end salons was through professional, full-service beauty distributors who sold exclusively in those markets. These big distributors had their own educators and sales teams and covered large territories—sometimes across several states.

I turned to a copy of the *Green Book*, an industry publication that listed all the distributors nationwide. Then I found a map and started cold calling. It was like trying to fit together a jigsaw puzzle, as I worked to align territories by geography.

Although putting this kind of distribution network together was certainly easier than traveling all over the country and recruiting salon owners to do that job, it was still painstakingly slow.

With hopes of making our mark as a recognized brand, we bought a booth at the Beauty and Barber Supply Institute (BBSI) trade show in Las Vegas the summer of 1989. There, we debuted our products and talked to distributors face-to-face. Despite being our competitor, my friend JP—John Paul DeJoria—graciously sent several potential distributors to our booth. We had a positive response and left feeling good about our new beginnings.

From the start, Dan had always emphasized the importance of having a written agreement explicitly outlining what our strategic vendors would provide. I'd already experienced more than my share of consequences from not having strong and clear agreements in place with my previous business partners. I took his advice seriously and went out of my way to cover every base. For example, Dan advised that we put in our agreements with chemistry labs a clause explicitly stating that should the lab go bankrupt, our formulas would be released to us and we would be excluded from the bankruptcy. Sure enough, that's exactly what happened with the lab we'd hired to produce ABBA products. Thankfully, Dan had provided the foresight that protected us, and that clause has been in every contract I've done since.

Another thing Dan helped me with was how to treat my team. As we ramped up at ABBA, we hired far more employees for the product side than I'd ever imagined previously. We created staff positions in advertising, marketing, public relations, education, logistics, sales, human resources, finance and operations. "In the motion picture industry, it's very important to keep your people," Dan said. "Given your business, I would think it's the same. Your people are your most important asset. Treat them fairly, so they stay with you."

I thought about his advice and worked to create a cohesive atmosphere where everyone knew their contributions were valued. I encouraged out-of-the-box thinking and kept an open-door policy. We served lunch nearly every day and kept the vibe positive and friendly.

Because I'd played so many different roles in the industry, I'd learned firsthand what was required for many of the jobs that were critical to our success. For example, some CEOs treat PR and marketing personnel as almost secondary, leaving them out of strategic executive meetings. But I believed that the people who were helping to tell our story and communicate our message properly were vitally important. I always gave them a seat at the table.

I aimed to treat all my employees the way Jay Sebring had treated me back when I'd first come to California hungry to learn and full of ideas. He'd encouraged my growth and taught me that asking the right questions and genuinely listening to the answers without being defensive is one of the most important skills needed to build healthy relationships—whether in business or in personal life.

Although ABBA Liquid Styling Tools delivered on the promised performance, we made three missteps with our launch. First, we did not have enough products in the line to meet all the variables of effectively caring for women's hair. Second, the packaging of the few products we had developed didn't look as good as they needed to on the shelves. Finally, we failed to communicate our exciting story properly.

On top of those issues, shortly after we started shipping product, we discovered something we'd never seen coming. A vendor was taking a counterfeit version of our formula, filling our bottles with it, and selling the bootleg product to salons. I thought about what my father had taught me years earlier: *Nobody likes a liar or a cheat*—especially not me. But in business, I'd also learned I couldn't afford to burn any bridges. There's never any benefit to keeping an enemies list. From that moment forward, I refused to waste time or energy on negativity.

Our initial sales were sluggish. We only generated about $800,000 in retail the first year.

As we balanced the books, I realized something needed to change. It seemed clear that our product's name—Liquid Styling Tools—had been a mistake. Although we'd had JP's permission to use the tagline, it presented ABBA as a copycat product instead of answering that all-important question: Why *this* product?

Our advertising had failed to tell our story in a powerful way, and our packaging had not made our bottles stand out in the saturated women's market.

If only I'd stood firm on the words "Pure and Natural," which clearly answered the question of "Why ABBA?" Yet again, I'd yielded to my partner even when I knew in my gut the better strategy.

The products we'd created were stellar—way beyond anything else on the market. We were 100 percent vegan—one of the first in our industry to go that direction. While many of our competitors were doing animal testing and using ingredients from animals at the time, we'd qualified for PETA's vegan and cruelty-free symbols. We'd also expanded the product line to include 10 different products, meeting more of the unique needs of our mostly female clients. But none of that mattered if women consumers weren't lured in by the packaging or our story.

By 1991, we'd nearly depleted our startup funds, and the little advertising we were doing wasn't working. I began to worry that my latest act was going to be a flop. One thing was certain—failure was not an option.

Unfortunately, things got worse. Because I was only drawing $500 a week in salary, the IRS declared that there was no way we could be living the lifestyle we had on that amount of money. Cheryl and I were audited. We had to prove that we'd been living on the $105,000 in savings that we'd managed to accumulate in the last years when we were in New Mexico. The frustrating process cost us time and money we didn't have, and by the time the IRS was finally satisfied, we were dangerously close to exhausting our savings.

We needed to reposition ABBA. That would mean draining the remaining seed money, but I was willing to make that bet. After convincing Alan and Dan that the marketing angle needed a change, we dropped the words "Liquid Styling Tools" from our name and we went with the tagline from my original business plan: "Pure and Natural."

Next, I met with our marketing, advertising, and public relations team. We collaborated to tell a more compelling story with cleaner copywriting, providing customers with answers to the crucial questions: Why THIS product? Why for me? Why NOW?

The new ABBA messaging focused on the fact that we made use of botanicals—roots, leaves, fruits, berries, and flowers—as well as essential oils in our products.

I'd tell customers, "You have a choice. You can use a product made from hooves, hides, and animal organs, or you can use a product that's made from roots, leaves, fruits, and flowers. The choice is yours."

That closed the deal every time.

Then I shelled out a healthy sum to a fashion photographer known for his work in high-fashion women's magazines. On the day of the shoot, the photographer guided us to a spot in the wetlands of Marina del Rey. He'd selected a setting on the coastline. The only issue was the prominent "No Trespassing" sign we crossed to reach the site.

"Don't worry about that," said the photographer, waving his hands. "We'll be in and out before anyone knows we were even here."

The young brunette model showed up wearing glasses and a frown. Alan had cut her thick hair, giving it a modern look that was gorgeous, but her dismal demeanor worried me, as it went against our brand's goal to make women look and feel their best. I asked her to take off her glasses, and the photo stylist put a large, carefully arranged bouquet of flowers in her hands.

In an instant, the model lit up for the camera. She looked innocent and natural, bathed in sunlight. It was pure magic. Electricity filled the air and I exhaled. I knew without a doubt that my gamble on spending so much on this photo shoot would prove to be the bold move that ABBA desperately needed.

I was right. The photographer caught those magical moments on film, and the soft, romantic full-color images were perfect for our brand. Now we had the proper "Why ABBA?" story that would speak to women with the lifestyle that we had targeted.

Next, we redesigned our packaging, adding bright colors to the white bottles. The industrial gray was gone, and the reaction was immediate. Consumers, salon owners, stylists, and distributors all loved these changes. Our products had always been great, but now we had a hip story that hit the right emotional notes. We also had the right timing, branding ourselves ahead of the trend of health consciousness and connecting with our customer's desire for more natural ingredients.

We'd known that breaking a new hair care product company into the crowded market would be tough, but we'd refused to quit. That first year, 103 new companies had taken part in the trade show. By the time we returned the following year, fewer than 10 of the 103 remained. Year three, only two returned—and that included ABBA. Thanks to hard work and a little help from our friends and family, we'd beaten the odds. ABBA had become a success, and not just a small success.

After the repositioning, our retail sales jumped to more than $4 million.

If I hadn't followed my gut instinct and taken action to rebrand the company, ABBA wouldn't have lasted much longer. This reinforced lessons I'd learned earlier: Follow your instincts.

Takeaways

- As a leader, create a culture where all employees feel valued.

- Become a master at listening and encourage your team members to share ideas with you.

- A lot of knowledge walks out the door when you lose good people.

- Always do your due diligence and get a minimum of three different vendors to bid for a job.

- Don't always accept the lowest bid. Use that as leverage to get the best vendor for the job.

- Document every communication and spell out everything clearly in agreements.

- Slow down to go fast.

- Asking the right questions and genuinely listening without being defensive is one of the most powerful tools you have in relationships—whether in business or personal life.

- Speak up for what you think is best, even if you're alone in your opinion.

INGREDIENT #19

BE PREPARED
FOR ANYTHING

We finally had a pretty big hit on our hands after repositioning ABBA Pure and Natural. By 1996, ABBA was making more money than I'd ever dreamed possible. We'd extended the brand to include more than 30 products, and we'd secured distribution in more than 4,000 salons across the country, reaching nearly every state.

After his initial excitement about ABBA's success wore off, Alan, who'd been handling the education side of the company, had grown increasingly tired of being on the road so much. Late in the third year, he insisted that his wife Gina, an attractive hair stylist, travel with him. He also wanted a limo to pick him up at the airport and take him to and from the show venues. He kept upping his demands to the point that some of the distributors were not happy with this.

Shortly after that revelation, Alan burst into my office to express his deep discontent. He argued that he should only do 10 shows a year because of the intensity of the travel.

At the peak of Markham, I'd been traveling more than half the year doing different appearances, shows, and other events. I tried to compromise, asking him to commit to at least 15 shows a year. But he refused.

"Well, if you're pulling back from the business, that means I'll be picking up the slack. I'll do it, but I deserve a salary increase for the additional work."

"No way," he responded. "I'm your equal partner and that's that."

I remained calm. I'd learned never to discuss business when emotions are high. "Let's talk more later," I suggested. Thankfully, he followed my lead.

Within a few months, he was back in my office. "I want a divorce. I want out of this relationship," he said.

"What? What are you talking about? ABBA is blowing up," I argued, sure he was just speaking from exhaustion.

He wrestled with his hands and spoke as if a huge weight was on his shoulders. "It's gotten to be too much, Markham. I want out."

I couldn't believe he really wanted to quit when we'd far exceeded anything we'd ever imagined possible. "Alan, what do you mean, you want out?"

"I want you to either buy me out or sell the company. I don't want to do this anymore."

I studied his face. His jaw was tense. He was serious.

As agreed in our original contract, I'd been carrying my weight managing the business, and he'd been doing his part in the education arm. Clearly, the pressure had become too much for him, and he was no longer happy. But we were on the verge of netting $25 million in retail sales and I was just hitting my stride.

My first thought was: *Maybe I could grow the company even more without a partner.*

"I'll look for a buyer," I said. "Let me get to work on it." Alan gave me a look, and then quietly walked out of my office.

At that same time, I'd been approached about being bought out by Styling Technology, a new company that had just gone public. Owned by

Sam Leopold, Styling Technology had an ambitious goal of rolling up various hair and beauty product lines into one large company—creating a one-stop shop for salon owners and stylists. And they'd already been reaching out to me with interest.

When Sam asked how much it would take to buy ABBA, I threw out a number. "I'd take $20 million," I said, not expecting that it would happen without intense negotiations. Within a little more than a week, we'd struck a deal. In 1997, ABBA was acquired by Styling Technology for my asking price of $20 million.

June 26, 1997

Dear Jim,

    In all the excitement of receiving these big dollars from the sale of Abba, I don't want to forget to express my appreciation and admiration for the wonderful job you did to make this all possible. I don't think it could have been possible without your special guidance and many hours of personal time you poured into the venture. To take $250,000 and turn it into $20,000,000 in such a short time is something to be proud of in the business world.

    In my wildest dreams, I never envisioned this ending, so take a well deserved bow and be assured that Arline and I am ever grateful for you efforts.

Sincerely,

Dan Genis

This time, our noncompete was a bit shorter—three years. That still seemed like an eternity to me, but it was better than the five-year clause I'd signed in the past. Additionally, the contract stipulated that we had to indemnify Styling Technology for any lawsuit that might arise within a year of the sale. We also maintained liability insurance that would cover us up to $1 million.

Soon after the sale, I found out that one of ABBA's distributors was unhappy that ABBA's new owner had cut him off. I called Sam and said, "Look, I think you can make this go away if you give him $20,000 or so. Honestly, I think he deserves it. He's been doing what he was supposed to be doing."

Sam laughed and said, "Hell no."

Sure enough, that lone distributor went to an attorney who advised him to find some other unhappy distributors and file a class action lawsuit for wrongful termination against Styling Technology. He rounded up another five distributors, and they filed a lawsuit for $20 million against the acquiring company.

Although we had not terminated any of our distributors and didn't cause any of the issues involved in the filing, we were on the hook for the lawsuit due to that indemnification clause.

We were all scared to death. We were in danger of losing everything even though we had done nothing wrong. I was powerless as the case dragged on for a year and a half. Sam cooperated with us and turned over boxes and boxes of corporate documents that covered up most of the space in our house. Many days and nights, Cheryl, who had given up her successful career in interior design, and I sifted through the paperwork, looking for any evidence that might possibly protect our position.

For more than a year, our lives were suspended in limbo, along with the lives of Alan, my father-in-law—who'd given us the seed investment—and Subhash Bahl, the chemist who'd helped us create the ABBA formulas. We had no idea how the case would be resolved, and we all felt as if that $20 million wasn't ours anymore. We could only wait and wonder if any of us would ever see a return on our investment in ABBA or if all of our hard work would be wiped out completely.

In the midst of all this drama, we got news that Cheryl was expecting a baby. We were over the moon. We'd been trying to get pregnant for several years, and we immediately started dreaming about what our lives would be like with an infant in the house. The pregnancy was a bright spot during such a tough time in our lives. Cheryl was by nature a nurturer who couldn't wait to become a mother, and I looked forward to being an older, wiser father this time around. So much had changed since I'd become a dad three times by age 22, and I was determined not to let this child grow up without me.

But four months into her pregnancy, Cheryl miscarried. We were devastated. We both believed that the stress from the lingering court case caused us to lose our baby. Once again, I struggled with feeling that everything was completely out of my control, as we grieved deeply for what might have been.

That was one of the most difficult times I've ever experienced. I began to think I wasn't meant to have anything good in my life. I also grew particularly frustrated with the slow pace of the court system. At one point, we brought in five of ABBA's distributors who were all happy and successful, and we gathered paperwork that boosted our case. However, the judge presiding over the arbitration refused to even look at the papers and wouldn't let a single one of the distributors testify on our behalf. "Who are these people?" he asked.

"Your Honor, they are ABBA distributors who are all happy with the company," our attorney said.

"Why would I want to hear from them? This case is about the unhappy distributors," he responded. "Get them out of my courtroom."

The process was maddening, and many times I was thankful I hadn't had to endure it as a younger, more temperamental man.

Finally, after nearly two years in arbitration, we settled for $2.2 million plus legal fees. Since our liability insurance only covered $1 million of that, each partner was expected to cover our respective shares of the remainder.

In the end, my father-in-law was content with the agreement, and we were all happy and relieved. And I took great pride in knowing I'd done something that hardly anybody ever does. I'd come back from the depths of hell yet again.

As I left the courtroom, the words of my old friend, Paul Newman, returned to me. Paul was right. I am Big Lucky.

Takeaways

- Make sure you have the right insurance policy in place when you sell.

- Read every word of your contract and pay close attention to any indemnity clauses.

- Avoid litigation if possible.

- Keep good records.

- Never underestimate the impact stress can have on your health.

INGREDIENT #20

ANSWER THE CALL

L ess than a year after we sold ABBA, Cheryl's best friend—Kerry Berk-Edelman—reached out to her. The two had met in elementary school, and Kerry had been Cheryl's roommate when she bought her first townhouse. As true friends do, Kerry and Cheryl had stayed in contact through the many years of relocations.

Once we'd left Albuquerque and moved to Orange County, Kerry and Cheryl made a point to meet about every six weeks, even though Kerry had moved to San Diego with her family. The two of them had been together for a week-long girls' retreat at a wellness spa in Ojai with their mothers when the phone call came.

The second Cheryl heard Kerry's voice, she knew something was wrong. "Cheryl, I've just come from my oncologist's office. I have ovarian cancer."

"Oh, Kerry," Cheryl said, stunned. "That can't be right. Surely they've made a mistake!"

"Unfortunately, there's no mistake," replied her friend.

"How can we help?" Cheryl asked, determined to make this easier in some way for her dear friend.

Kerry told her that her doctor had given her a long list of do-not-use ingredients in the personal care products she'd been using.

Cheryl called me over and handed me a list that had just been faxed over by Kerry. When I got on the phone with her, I calmly asked her, "Why don't you just use ABBA?"

"I can't," she said. "Some of the ingredients are on the do-not-use list."

That caught me completely by surprise. We'd built the entire brand around natural products that were the safest on the market.

Kerry was an energetic, fun-loving woman with a great sense of humor. She wore her thick, curly brunette hair in a bob and was always on-the-go, usually wearing sports clothes as she dashed about town. Once her twin boys were born, she'd become even more committed to a healthy lifestyle. She shopped exclusively at natural food stores and centered her life around wellness. I'd always enjoyed her down-to-earth, direct approach to life and couldn't believe she, of all people, had been diagnosed with cancer. Despite this terrible news she'd just received, she remained optimistic and eager to find practical solutions that would help extend her life.

"I'll look at the list closely," I said. "I'm sure we can come up with something."

As careful as I'd been in creating what I thought were healthy options for consumers, I was shocked to see that only three out of ABBA's 30 products didn't contain ingredients on the personal care do-not-use list from Kerry's doctor. And none of those three products were shampoo or conditioner.

The longer Cheryl and I pored over the list, the more alarmed I grew. Kerry was right. The do-not-use list was overwhelming, with more than 20 ingredients deemed unsafe.

There was no time to waste. I went to work right away. I called my chemist friend, Subhash Bahl, and shared the list with him. We started figuring out alternative ingredients, determined to create a clean and safe shampoo and conditioner for Kerry. I felt the full weight of the urgency of this mission: Kerry was like a sister to Cheryl. She was family. And time was ticking.

Subhash and I worked closely together, first on the shampoo. In particular, sulfates jumped out at me. They were in a vast number of beauty products and in virtually all shampoos on the market, because they're cleansing agents that create lather. But I learned they can also cause skin irritation and sometimes contain traces of 1,4-Dioxane, a suspected carcinogen that forms during the production of the shampoo. Sulfates were typically the second ingredient listed after water in shampoos.

Now a big motivator had been presented to me. Because I'd been working with ingredients for a long time and had developed more than 100 products, and because Subhash was a curious scientist who was eager to discover new ingredients, we came up with seven different surfactants that were not sulfates. After multiple rounds of testing and revisions over a couple of months, we developed a revolutionary new shampoo. It was vegan, like ABBA's product had been, but this time the formula was sulfate-free and salt-free. Despite the absence of sulfate and salt, the shampoo maintained a tremendous lather, rinsed well, and left the hair shiny and smooth. Best of all, it was free of all of the ingredients the oncologist instructed Kerry not to use.

Once I was satisfied with the performance, I added a signature blend of aromatherapy essences with a top note of patchouli. As soon as we finished perfecting the shampoo, we deployed the same process to come up with a unique formula for a safe conditioner.

We eagerly awaited Kerry's feedback. She called me as soon as she used her new products. "Jim, this feels luxurious," she said. "I love the way it leaves my hair feeling. And to top it off, it smells heavenly. Thank you so much. I love it."

She ran my formulas by her doctor, who gave us a stamp of approval.

Despite our best efforts and her valiant fight, our beautiful friend Kerry died on January 27, 1998. Our hearts were all broken.

Kerry's diagnosis was a serious wake-up call and helped me see what I'd formulated in the lab could have long-lasting impact on people's health. As a result, Cheryl and I discovered our true mission in the aftermath of Kerry's death. We began supporting City of Hope—one of the nation's foremost cancer research and treatment centers, where Kerry had received cutting-edge therapies and compassionate care.

As we met more families facing cancer, we listened to their stories and felt called to play a more active role. We just weren't sure yet what our role would be. One night, still grieving the loss of our friend, we were discussing how unfair cancer can be to steal someone as healthy and active as Kerry had been, such a vibrant and loving mother with young children, someone who was so determined to live.

"It makes me realize how short life really is," Cheryl said. "I mean, who knows how much time any of us have left in this world?"

I listened as she worked through the loss, trying to channel her pain into something positive.

"We've been given so many opportunities, Jim. And you've worked so hard to improve people's lives along the way. But this has me wanting to do more," she said. "I want to use every minute we have left to do good in the world—to really improve people's lives and try to prevent one more child from having to bury their mother."

That night, as emotions surfaced, so did ideas. We decided to further our research on the products we'd developed for Kerry. If we could share these safer products with consumers, maybe we could reduce the number of people facing such devastating battles with cancer. At the very least, maybe we could provide these products to cancer patients and cancer survivors, reaching them through doctors' offices and health food stores where these products might also appeal to other health-conscious consumers.

During one of our saddest moments, we discovered our life's work.

In April 1999, fueled by our love for Kerry, Cheryl and I attended Cosmoprof Worldwide Bologna. It was held in the beautiful Northern Italian city that dated back to the sixth century A.D. Our goal was to honor Kerry's legacy and create a new line of products that contained no carcinogens. In order to do that, we needed to learn the latest in hair care and beauty on the international front, where natural products were more commonly used.

The experience proved overwhelming. Models demonstrated products at every turn, and companies competed for attention with each display more glamourous than the next. Some threw fancy cocktail parties; others provided hair demonstrations and free samples. The overall effect was sensory overload, and that energy brought us both back to life again.

Having received such positive feedback while conducting small-scale testing on Kerry's products, we concentrated our efforts on studying different hair care, color, and natural product companies. What we discovered was totally unexpected. There was a worldwide color boom going on. Everything was all about color. Universally, all the color companies were seeing 20–30 percent increases year after year in their business.

Through the initial feedback, it became clear that the product we'd created for Kerry helped keep color in.

"What if we still concentrate on creating healthy products, but emphasize that our product holds color?" I asked. I looked at Cheryl, and she looked back at me.

"It is a bigger market," she said, smiling.

"Honey, I believe we could make this even more successful than ABBA."

Over dinner that first night, Cheryl and I could barely contain our excitement. We were both on the same page and brimming with ideas.

Especially because just before we'd left for Italy, we'd been notified that Styling Technology had declared bankruptcy. That meant I was no longer bound by the noncompete. I was free to begin again.

Next, we went to Paris, where we stumbled across a store called Sephora—the biggest beauty store we'd ever seen. The location on the Champs-Élysées was open from 10:00 a.m. until 2:00 a.m., and shoppers appeared at all hours. We looked at the trends and watched what customers were buying. We studied what they picked up from the shelves and quizzed store clerks on what patterns they noticed from the shoppers. Curious, we went back at different times each day to see who was shopping when. Most of all, we examined the ingredients list. We discovered that certain products stood out to customers. We also noted certain marketing strategies that seemed to be effective.

We bought so many products, we had to buy an extra suitcase to get them home.

Immediately upon our return, we scoured the US market looking for products that were designed to protect hair color. The only product we found was in the mass retail market in grocery stores and drugstores. It was called ColorVive and was made by the French hair care and beauty giant L'Oréal.

"We may be dead in the water," I said. "They're probably already working on something similar for the professional market."

We were determined to find out.

We learned that ColorVive was one of L'Oréal's top-selling lines. After talking to several distributors and hearing that there wasn't even a whisper about L'Oréal coming out with a color protection line for the pros, I was left unsettled.

"Why wouldn't they be going into this market when ColorVive is doing so well?" I asked. If the biggest beauty and hair care product company in the world was ignoring this niche, maybe we were missing something.

Meanwhile, Subhash and I kept working on different formulations to improve their color protection factor. We conducted a lot of exploratory meetings and gathered more than 20 people with all kinds of hair types and hair colors to test our new formulas. Cheryl was one of the testers. She tried every new product on her mid-length honey blonde hair and swore we'd struck gold.

Once we determined to a degree of certainty that L'Oréal wasn't planning to enter the professional market with a color-protection line, we decided to move forward full force. In many ways, the fact that L'Oréal wasn't pursuing the market made pioneering the concept seem far riskier. But I've always been a risk-taker, and I was ready for a new challenge.

All my years in the industry had given me an excellent network of experts to draw upon in every area in which we needed help. We pulled in some of the professionals who'd been with us at ABBA, and others I'd known from Markham and in my Sebring days. Collaboration would be key.

Over the next nine months, we spent entire days with top experts, listening to their advice regarding bottling, branding, graphic design, packaging, marketing, advertising, and every aspect of the business. I wanted to hear multiple viewpoints and consider the best options available every step of the way.

We devoted hours to discussing how our product should feel, who we were appealing to, what age of woman we would target, and the best way to deliver our message. This process took time and a lot of effort, but the collaborative team we pulled together shared our excitement. We were creating a whole new category: color care. And more importantly, the entire line was made from non-toxic ingredients. We were developing something revolutionary for the entire industry, and the energy among us was intensely positive.

Some of the liveliest brainstorming sessions were built around what to name this new company. We wanted to be known for healthy, clean, high-performing products that had been carefully formulated with the highest quality ingredients. We worked together to find the perfect name for our new brand.

Finally, the team agreed to meld two words: *pure*, which is what our products were, and *ology*, which is the Greek word for science.

Together, the name was PureOlogy—the science of pure.

"That's it," I said. "That's exactly what we're about."

Takeaways

- When life hands you a bigger mission, answer the call.

- If you're down, rally the hero inside you and use your pain to fuel you forward.

- Whatever you set your mind to, give your very best effort and use the best talent to help you.

- When others sense your passion, they'll be more willing to take the plunge with you.

- Do your research and let the best idea win.

- The narrower the focus, the wider the potential.

- Listen to other ideas and give credit where credit is due.

INGREDIENT #21

WISH HARD,
BUT WORK HARDER

Everything was coming together for PureOlogy Serious Colour Care—our professional line of products designed exclusively for colorists and their clients. We invested time up front researching every little detail and carefully curating the best team of professionals so that we could give our customers a valuable, new experience. For instance, having learned from earlier mistakes, I wanted the bottles to be special. I'd looked around at the industry, but hadn't found anything that inspired me. Then, while Cheryl and I were on a wine tour in Napa Valley, I saw an olive oil bottle with a long neck. It stood out from the rest and caught my eye. That became my inspiration for the shape of the PureOlogy bottles.

We wanted our advertising to be unique, too. With PureOlogy, we had a great story to tell about our radically different formulas—the first professional, sulfate-free line exclusively designed to protect color-treated hair and hold color longer. That concept was revolutionary. The brand deserved an equally creative and effective ad campaign that would position PureOlogy properly with customers and with stylists.

The typical advertising in the beauty industry featured a gorgeous female model with beautiful hair. We tried something different. We ran a series of ads spotlighting various items that are known to fade such as blue jeans, photographs, memories, newspapers. For each item, we added a corresponding tagline: *Jeans fade, your hair color shouldn't*. It proved to be a very effective campaign, and one that still makes me smile today.

We also tapped some of our previous ABBA distributors to begin distributing PureOlogy. The first weekend of September 2001, Cheryl and I traveled to the Waldorf-Astoria in New York to attend a gala for People for the Ethical Treatment of Animals (PETA). Paul McCartney and Pat Benatar were both honored that night for their efforts to protect all forms of life, and we were inspired by their generous activism. While in the city, we also joined our New York distributor for a successful launch party for our new product line.

We had a wonderful weekend and then boarded a plane to return to LA on September 10. Our plane kept getting delayed due to a terrible thunderstorm. We finally took off late that evening, one of the last flights out of JFK. We'd barely gotten into bed back in Orange County and fallen asleep when our phone kept ringing. When I finally answered, Cheryl's brother Guy was on the line.

"Thank God, you're home. Turn on the TV."

Confused, I asked, "What? Why?"

"Just turn on the TV," he said, clearly upset.

I switched on the television to see 9/11 unfolding. Cheryl and I watched in horror, simultaneously acknowledging that we could have easily been on one of those flights. Cold chills ran through me as we realized yet again how quickly life can change. September 11 has since served as an annual reminder, helping me to never take a single day for granted and to always express gratitude for the time we're given.

I'd learned early in life that it's important to surround ourselves with the right people. I'd also learned that sometimes people will disappoint us, betray us, or even try to hurt us intentionally. For that reason, I've always tried to reward kindhearted people who have a strong work ethic. Throughout my career, some have stood out more than others.

One day, I discovered a terrific distributor named John Maly. When we launched PureOlogy, I started him out with just one territory, but I soon realized that he was a powerhouse. I followed my gut and gave him the lucrative Orange County territory. My bet on him paid off. Before long, I assigned him additional territories and eventually PureOlogy represented 20 percent of Maly's west coast business. By 2007, Maly's distributorship alone generated $40 million in sales to salons.[2]

While Maly was soaring, I'd grown increasingly unhappy with the big distributor who'd been handling PureOlogy in Pennsylvania. I didn't feel like he was giving the line the attention it deserved. About that time, a young man named John Philipp called me out of the blue. His small, family owned company distributed products and he wanted my business.

"Look, Mr. Markham, I'll work harder for you than you can imagine," he said. "I'll do everything I can to make PureOlogy the top brand in this market."

I thought about how Jay Sebring had taken a chance on me. I also thought about my frustrations with my current Pennsylvania distributor. The choice was easy. "John, I'm going to give you the PureOlogy distributorship."

He made good on his promise and quickly became one of the most successful distributors. His company went from three employees to 51 in just four years.

I also made good on my promise to my son Jay. He'd grown tired of his job in the oil industry and became the PureOlogy distributor for Oklahoma. He thrived in that position. Not only had all three of my children taken back my name, by that time they'd all elected to be in the hair industry.

For the first two years, we spent a lot of time educating stylists, teaching *why* sulfate-free products were safer and *why* they were superior for color-treated hair. Once again, we'd created a revolutionary new product—the first sulfate-free, salt-free product line in the industry, and one with a compelling story and marketing strategy.

More importantly, with steady profits coming in, our platform had given us an opportunity to bring attention to the groundbreaking work of the City of Hope and the National Ovarian Cancer Coalition. By sharing Kerry's story, we could play a small part in funding more research on ovarian cancer, which often goes undetected until it's already reached late stage.

In honor of Kerry, Cheryl began overseeing our philanthropic efforts and devoted tremendous time and energy to this important cause. By emphasizing the health benefits of sulfate-free products, we ended up sparking a worldwide shift. Within a decade, sulfate-free formulas became the standard for professional hair care manufacturers who opted to remove sodium laureth sulfate and sodium lauryl sulfate due to their harsh side effects. The sulfate-free movement quickly extended to beauty and personal care products too, with everything from toothpaste to laundry detergent ditching the toxic ingredient.

When I'd first contacted Subhash Bahl to find a safer product for Kerry, I could have never foreseen all that would happen in the years to follow. I'd simply given my best efforts to help Kerry, with no intentions of building a company around that idea. Looking back now, Cheryl and I can see the tremendous impact Kerry's life had on this groundbreaking shift to develop safer products for millions of consumers. None of this would have happened if she hadn't fought valiantly against cancer and had the foresight to find alternative solutions to the products that had been available at the time of her diagnosis.

We ended up winning the HBA Global Packaging award our second year in business. *Health, Allure,* and *Vogue* all named PureOlogy as *Best Shampoo* that year, too. By the end of year three, we were growing at such a fast pace and had such a hold on the market share that I got a phone call from a broker putting a feeler out for a potential investor.

The matchmaker put me in contact with Chuck Esserman, founder of TSG Consumer Partners, a private equity firm out of San Francisco. Chuck had an outstanding reputation for partnering with visionary entrepreneurs and helping them grow their brands. He flew to meet Cheryl and me at our office.

A graduate of MIT with an MBA from Stanford, Chuck was a

thoughtful listener who asked a lot of intelligent questions. We had a beautifully packaged, perfectly positioned product line that was addressing an unmet need in color, which represented 75% of the market for women at salons. He seemed particularly impressed that I had such an in-depth knowledge of every aspect of the business. For example, when he asked about financials, I was able to give him details by account, by distributor, and by product.

I gave him the highlights of my story and how I'd developed comprehensive knowledge of so many aspects of the hair care industry.

"So, you've done this multiple times," he asked. "And you've had to learn everything on your own?"

"Well, I've had some good mentors along the way," I explained. "But you're correct in that I've hardly had any formal education to speak of."

After spending the day with us at our Irvine, California, headquarters, Chuck said, "What you've put together here is extraordinary, Jim and Cheryl. You have a great partnership, and I can see how you complement each other."

TSG bought in as an investment partner to help us handle all the demands that our rapid growth was putting on our company. Despite our vastly different backgrounds, Chuck and I both shared a gift for finding ways to do things better and differently. We hit it off, and so did Cheryl and his wife Ivette.

In addition to getting Chuck as an advisor, I also got TSG's Yasser Toor—a brilliant strategist in his late 20s. Yasser met with me regularly to offer ideas and serve as a sounding board. He was impressed by the family atmosphere among our staff.

From working with Chuck and Yasser, I learned better structure and a higher level of business management. They taught me new ways to analyze opportunities and trends—all while having fun doing it.

One afternoon after back-to-back meetings, Yasser said, "I've never met another CEO like you. You manage to look at things at a macro level as well as a micro level. Your approach is totally different from what they teach at business school, but it works."

Chuck and Yasser brought me in on deals for two other hair care companies in TSG's portfolio: Alterna and Sexy Hair. Eventually, they asked me to take over as Alterna's CEO. For about a year, I split my time between Alterna and PureOlogy, spending two days a week at Alterna and three at PureOlogy.

Unfortunately, what had worked beautifully at PureOlogy wasn't making much of a difference at Alterna, which was in a turnaround situation at the time — the corporate equivalent of a deeply dysfunctional family. At PureOlogy, I'd worked hard to create a collaborative, family-style relationship based on trust and respect with our employees. We'd succeeded in business because we all stood united on our mission and our goals. Alterna's work environment proved challenging because trust had been broken within the ranks. I was an outsider met with suspicion, and my hands-on style of asking a ton of questions was about as well received as when I'd taken over for Jay at Sebring International.

As a result of the added tension, my health suffered and I gained weight. I was running myself ragged trying to apply the winning formula I'd established at PureOlogy to this new-to-me company, and nothing I tried seemed to be working.

About a year into it, Chuck called. "Jim, I'm concerned about you," he said. "With the way you operate, I think asking you to split your focus between PureOlogy and Alterna was a mistake on our part. We want you to put all your focus back on PureOlogy."

"You know I never like to walk away from a challenge," I said. "But I know that my biggest successes have come when I've been laser-focused on one big goal. PureOlogy is at a critical point, and I believe we can make it one of the biggest brands out there."

Once I went back to focusing solely on PureOlogy, my health improved and the company's growth tripled. PureOlogy was becoming very successful, with trademarks filed in 35 countries as we prepared to take PureOlogy international.

Since we gained so much inspiration from Paris, Cheryl and I returned there each spring and would sometimes squeeze in a second visit in the late summer or fall. One day, while walking along the streets of Paris, a beautiful window display of L'Oréal products caught Cheryl's eye. She stopped, grabbed my arm and said, "Can you just imagine that whole rack right there being PureOlogy?"

We both took a moment to picture the scenario. The seed was planted.

As the year progressed, we talked about what we wanted for the next stage in our lives. We both wanted more time to travel, and we agreed that we'd explore the possibility of selling the company.

In March 2007, TSG Consumer Partners put out feelers for a buyer. Within a week, we had a dozen companies interested. Over several days we put our best foot forward for all 12 suitors. Five strong offers came in.

Cheryl and I returned to Paris Easter of 2007. We also arranged to meet with Sephora executives while there and were delighted to hear their enthusiasm about carrying PureOlogy in their European Union stores.

When we returned to our hotel, an urgent message was waiting for us. A top executive from L'Oréal asked that we hold off on any further talks with Sephora. The message we received said, "Please don't sell anything to Sephora. We want to buy your company."

"How did they even know we were here?" Cheryl asked, stunned.

Equally surprised, I said simply, "I have no idea."

With PureOlogy, we had lightning in a bottle: the best distributors, the best formulas, the best staff, the best partners. Everything had come together perfectly. And at that point the company was flowing and flourishing—on track to do more than $263 million in retail sales in 2007, up from $200 million in 2006.

Although L'Oréal had offered less money than other bidders, they'd agreed to do something that was vitally important to me: my freedom. I didn't want to work for anyone else. I also wanted a short non-compete, just in case I decided retirement wasn't for me.

L'Oréal agreed to the deal with that short non-compete. May 8th, 2007, PureOlogy was sold for $280 million. All cash.

At a celebratory dinner at Mastro's Steakhouse near our Orange County home, I told the executives from L'Oréal how close we'd come to not starting the company due to their successful consumer brand ColorVive. "Cheryl and I couldn't figure out why you weren't in the professional market, and we were worried that you knew something we didn't," I confessed.

The vice president of L'Oréal exchanged a look with the other senior executive. He shrugged his shoulders and said, "We just missed it."

Once again, I realized how narrow the margin can be when it comes to success. We could have easily delayed our timing and missed the narrow window for PureOlogy. Thankfully, we followed our instincts and pursued the project with a passion fueled all along by our love for Kerry and our desire to honor her life.

After the news of the sale broke, Sephora heavily pursued me to produce an exclusive Jim Markham line of products for its EU stores. I was flattered, but it was a no-go for me at that point. I was content traveling with Cheryl and enjoying more time together with the people I loved. We took our entire family—children, grandchildren, and friends John and Denise Philipp—on a cruise to Alaska.

As if we hadn't already felt like winners after the sale, that year was capped off by a slew of awards. One of the greatest moments of my life was being recognized as Ernst & Young's 2007 *Entrepreneur of the Year* in the Consumer Retail Products category for the region covering California, Nevada, and Arizona. To be considered, you had to have been in business five years and had a 20-percent increase in sales every year plus a 20-percent increase in your EBITDA each year.

When our category was announced, I admit I sank a bit in disappointment when I didn't place. It wasn't that I needed the award, but the recognition would have validated all those years of persistence in the face of failures and acknowledged the value of devoting ourselves to the pursuit of excellence. Little did I know I'd been named the overall winner of our category!

As the shock wore off and I rose to accept my award, I was taken back to the first Roffler Razor-Cutting National Championship competition, when I stood with my old friend Bill and didn't even realize we'd won the grand championship until he nudged me toward the stage. Life had brought me full circle, and I'd learned so much. While accepting the honor, I saluted the young courageous teen who had always refused to quit. *You did it, Jim,* I thought to myself. *You beat the odds and broke the dysfunctional cycles and made all your dreams come true.*

Takeaways

- Reward kindhearted people who have strong work ethic.

- When someone isn't doing a good job, you need to reevaluate.

- Surround yourself with people who match your work ethic and style.

- When you feel you aren't able to be you at your best, listen, adjust, refuel, take a break. Do whatever you need to do to get back on track.

- Know yourself well enough to know what will make you happy.

- Recognize when you've got lightning in a bottle.

- You can't *wish* yourself to success. You can *dream* about it, but that won't get you there either. It takes hard work, detailed preparation and the right team at your side.

INGREDIENT #22

ADD COLOR

It was fitting that the last two decades of my professional career have been all about color. Why do I love color? It's a way to express individuality. Color can be bold, creative, fun, dramatic, chic, understated, wild, elegant—whatever you want it to be. It makes a statement.

The products we create are all about preserving, protecting, and enhancing color. In examining what role I play in the world at large, I've come to view those as my primary functions as well—PRESERVING the environment, PROTECTING the future for our children, and ENHANCING the lives of those within my sphere of influence.

In the first half of my career, I'd functioned mostly in survival mode. Once we became profitable, Cheryl took charge of the philanthropy, while I focused on growth and development.

After Kerry's cancer, suddenly my purpose expanded beyond the business of helping our clients feel beautiful. The drive to develop products that were clean of potentially harmful chemicals became embedded in our corporate culture and mission.

As a company, we were committed to raising awareness of ovarian cancer and supporting the work of City of Hope. But then something happened that expanded our scope even further.

Moved by the tragedy that Hurricane Katrina left in its wake, Vidal Sassoon invited Cheryl and me to a fundraiser called Hairdressers Unlocking Hope. Vidal and Mary Rector, from Behind the Chair, were heading up the event. They asked those in attendance to join them in funding and building houses through Habitat for Humanity.

I was the first to stand up. "We'll match you and donate enough to build two houses," I said. I pledged $88,000 for each house. Only later did I learn that we were expected to join Vidal in Louisiana and help with the construction.

"Are you sure about this, Cheryl?" I asked, explaining my concerns.

"Absolutely," she said, always eager to elevate others. "If Vidal wants us to help him in Louisiana, then that's what we'll do."

So, in 2006 and 2007, a small group of us descended on Slidell, Louisiana, a suburb about 30 miles north of New Orleans. There, we worked with a chapter of Habitat for Humanity. Vidal, who had devoted himself to philanthropy after selling his company, had raised a total of $1.7 million from the community of beauty and hair professionals—enough to build 21 houses. We made four different trips down there, which concluded when we presented recipients the keys to their new homes.

I had long admired Vidal ever since I'd shared a stage with him at a 1968 hair show in Dallas, but I'd never spent much time with him until we met up again in Louisiana. Working side-by-side, seeing him in action and the joy and caring he brought to the selfless project touched me deeply.

When I joked that two hair stylists wouldn't be worth much on a construction site, Vidal smiled and said, "We're both in the business of helping people feel better. This is just another way to do that."

It didn't take me long to realize he was one of the kindest and smartest men I'd ever met.

With a team of dedicated volunteers, we worked together tirelessly in the hot, humid southern heat until the construction of two new homes were finished. Both houses were for single moms who also worked hand in hand with us on the project. Watching their children's excitement as they walked through their new homes was priceless to both Cheryl and me.

Vidal and I bonded through this experience. Slowly, we discovered that we'd led parallel lives in many ways—even dating back to our rough starts as children. Like Paul Newman, Vidal served as a great example of generosity in my life and became a trusted friend.

As we handed the keys to those new homeowners, Paul's wise advice came back to me: "Be like the farmer. Put more seeds in than you take out." Paul had gone on to bring that generosity of spirit to his own special brand of philanthropy, insisting he didn't want to *put his face on something* unless it could help somebody else.

With that goal in mind, he created Newman's Own, donating 100 percent of the profits to charities that went along with his commitment to making the world a better place.

Working in New Orleans side-by-side with families who had lost everything in the storm helped me realize what Paul had known all along—how wonderful it feels to serve others. From that moment forward, I decided to model my life after good, kind, generous men like Vidal Sassoon and Paul Newman. I vowed to never forget my humble roots, and to always aim to give more than I take.

Less than a year after we sold PureOlogy, seller's remorse began to set in. Right about the time we were wondering what our next step should be, we were asked to be City of Hope *Spirit of Life* honorees and raise money for its annual fundraiser. For a full year, starting in mid-2008, Cheryl and I pushed aside any business goals and focused exclusively on City of Hope.

We hired a full-time staff to help, including my son Bobby. Together, we threw our hearts and souls into the project, filming a PSA for City of Hope and hosting the gala in July 2009. It was an exceptional evening, hailed as a meaningful and inspiring event for all. In addition to what we'd personally contributed to the campaign, we raised $1.3 million—a substantial undertaking considering we didn't have a corporation behind us to help with the effort.

We were still riding that high when just 10 weeks later, Cheryl was diagnosed with a rare form of lymphoma in the joints of her knees. Our worst fears took hold as we remembered Kerry's painful battle ending without a cure. I immediately called the oncologist reputed to be the best in Orange County, but I was devastated to learn we couldn't even get an appointment for three months. Then we remembered our friends at City of Hope. One phone call later, we were seeing a top specialist the following day.

When we walked in the room, Cheryl's new oncologist turned out to be the exact doctor we had cast to star in our PSA. We knew at that moment that this was no coincidence. Destiny had guided us the whole way.

Starting around the Christmas holidays, Cheryl had chemo and radiation treatments, but ironically, the precise type she needed, Rituxin, was invented by her doctor, Stephen Forman, and his research team at City of Hope. Miraculously, Cheryl did not lose any hair. After a year of treatments, surrounded by a supportive circle of loved ones and prayer, Cheryl beat cancer. Never before had I felt more blessed by God and never before more grateful.

After Cheryl's full recovery, we began traveling extensively with family and friends. It didn't take long before we found ourselves looking at hair care products and popping into salons in whatever city we were touring.

Former distributors and salon owners would ask, "What are you going to do for an encore?"

More importantly, Cheryl and I were asking ourselves that same question.

During a trip to Paris with our friends and former distributors John and Denise Philipp, the topic of conversation kept rolling around to when we were going to gear up again. John, who had lost his business when we sold PureOlogy, took a sip of wine and said, "You make the best hair products on the planet, Jim. You can't be finished yet. The industry needs innovation."

By the time we came home with yet another suitcase full of products, Cheryl and I knew that retirement wasn't in the cards for us.

We'd stayed abreast of advancements in ingredient technology and knew that just as with electronics or any other product, what was good 10 years ago no longer was good enough. I wanted the chance to improve what I started.

I had become even more passionate about formulas and knowing exactly what should go in them. I knew the 150+ key ingredient manufacturers around the world and had stayed connected with many of them as well as perfumers with the finest essential oils. Rather than let them introduce ingredients to us through our lab—which is the way most hair care companies operate—we proactively sought them out. I was determined to get the absolute best and most effective ingredients available.

I went back to the drawing board, once again working with my friend and chemist Subhash Bahl. My goal was to create a shampoo and conditioner that topped the best-selling formulas—even better than those we developed for PureOlogy. Subhash took the challenge personally to create carcinogen-free product, because he'd also been suffering the reoccurrence of cancer.

After our noncompete was up in 2010, we began working on the product line for our new company.

Sadly, Subhash died of cancer before we launched. I grieved the loss of yet another friend to this horrible disease, and I grew more determined than ever to bring safer products to consumers worldwide.

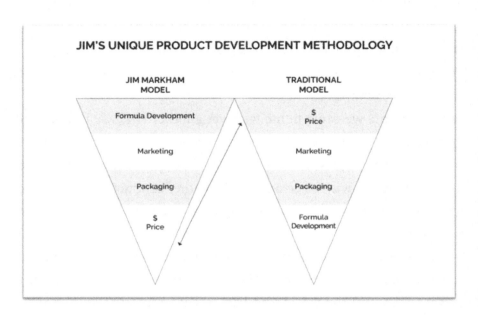

By the time, we re-entered the market with our new company, ColorProof Color Care Authority, the distribution had shifted to what's called a "multi-channel market." With e-commerce booming, our distributors were now selling through their own websites and stores. Still, for our best-of-class, groundbreaking products, professional distributors remained the powerbrokers for us.

John and Denise Philipp of TruBeauty Concepts were the first distributorship we awarded for ColorProof. Many of our primary ColorProof distributors, like Gino Barbo of Salon Service Group, Steve Cohn of Premier Beauty, and David and Al DiTullio of A & A Beauty Supplies had been with us during PureOlogy, and some had even stuck with us from as early as the ABBA days. Like my father-in-law always said, "Keep your good people with you."

At Cosmoprof Las Vegas 2011, we handed out lab samples for ColorProof's first 11 products to potential distributors. We were met with a fantastic reception, and our excitement over our new company hit a fever pitch. After my son Bobby's stint with us working on the City of Hope fundraiser, he was one of our first hires for ColorProof, and he opened up most of our distributors. He's now our regional sales manager.

ColorProof represented the culmination of all the lessons I'd learned as an entrepreneur—we use only the highest-quality, most cutting-edge ingredients, and we don't let cost factor into it.

After the successful launch of ColorProof, we created another break-through system called BioRepair-8, a drug-free formula designed to help prevent hair loss. BioRepair-8 uses safe and effective natural ingredients including alpha hydroxy fruit acids and apple stem cells. When young consumers learned how our system of preventative care would guard against hair thinning and hair loss, BioRepair-8 became our fastest seller.

As we move into a "super clean" era, our newest breakthrough yet is ColorProof's SuperSheer System, featuring the first silicone-free, fragrance-free, and hypoallergenic products for color-treated hair.

Our focus remains on providing clean, non-toxic, environmentally-friendly vegan products for our consumers, while maintaining superior results.

In recent years, we've paid more attention to the environmental impact as well, using a percentage of recycled plastics for our bottles. Additionally, our labels are now produced with eco-friendly inks and the labels easily peel off to be fully recyclable. Our target is to have all of our packaging 100 percent recycled and recyclable in the very near future.

Trends are always changing. Market channels change. Competition changes. The way people communicate changes. So how can a company stay relevant in a constantly shifting landscape? My secret: Be relentlessly curious.

I'm always observing and asking questions that some might consider off the wall and impossible to answer. When I'm developing a product, I start with the basic questions like *who is it for? What do we want it to do? What's the point of difference?* But the next round of questions are designed to push the limits and spark out-of-the-box thinking.

At ColorProof, we've created a culture of risk-taking. We encourage our team members to brainstorm, and we let them know that it's okay to try new things. Our company culture is centered around the belief that failure isn't fatal, and sometimes risk has a big payoff.

When it comes to the next big idea, I say *nothing is impossible*. It didn't seem possible for this uneducated, impoverished young barber from a desert oil town to go to Hollywood and launch an average of one company per decade—each different and each ahead of its time. But that's exactly what I've done my entire career: I've made the impossible possible. Never forget:

WE ARE ALL MADE TO WIN.

Takeaways

- Add color to the world and make other people's lives better.

- Success without giving back is not success.

- Honor your roots. Aim for the sky.

- Have faith.

- Every day counts.

- Some "wins" mean more than others.

- Stay curious.

- Dream big, and work to make your dream a reality.

YOU HAVE EVERYTHING
YOU NEED TO SUCCEED

T urns out, Paul Newman was right: I am Big Lucky. But I think there's a little more to my story than luck. My success has been a culmination of hard work, courage, and a determination to try new things.

I believe anyone can succeed. You simply have to refuse to quit, against all odds, and you have to choose to declare yourself a winner, even if the rest of the world hasn't seen it yet. You must first believe in yourself no matter what. Positive thinking was critical in my life. If you believe you can win, you can.

In other words, it's not just the lucky few who can make their dreams come true. It's everyone with grit, work ethic, resilience, curiousity, passion, and the right partner.

I've also learned that while awards and successes mean a lot to me, what's really important is a place to belong and a life of love filled with friends and family.

While my business success has given us a wonderful life, it's my wife, Cheryl, and my three children—Vickie, Bobby, and Jay—and our grandchildren—Tyson, Chandler, and Leslie—who've been my greatest blessings.

A lot has transpired in the intervening months since wrapping up the final chapters of *Big Lucky.* The world found itself in the throes of the Covid-19 crisis, and mandated closures in California meant I had to make some expeditious decisions about what would be best for the health of our company—ColorProof—and the wellbeing of our employees.

In early April 2020, I worked to secure funding to protect the salaries of our employees through the government Paycheck Protection Program (PPP), renegotiated the lease on our offices, and pivoted the company from a typical office environment to a remote workforce.

One month later, I as approached by long-time collaborator Bob Clark—owner of Cosway, our laboratory partner—and Cosway President Rick Hough with an unsolicited, all-cash offer to buy ColorProof. I have known Bob and Rick since we began working together during the Abba days.

Still, it took more than two weeks of careful consideration while quarantined at my home in Hawaii to agree to the sale. I felt that the sale would be good for the company and would allow me to pursue my budding passion for more personal mentoring and teaching others that they, too, are *made to win.*

Since the sale, I have been able to devote a greater portion of my time to virtual appearances, podcasts, and promotion of *Big Lucky.* Who knows what else the future will bring?

Perhaps Cheryl said it best when she looked at me recently and said, "Jim, you've got no quit in you."

In just that short sentence, she managed to capture the essence of my entire career.

If an uneducated, impoverished young man from Farmington, New Mexico can achieve the kind of success I've found in my life, then I'll end by saying what I said from the start: You can do absolutely anything with your life. Why? Because you were *made to win*. As Thomas Edison said, "Our greatest weakness lies in giving up." The most certain way to succeed is always try just one more time.

Takeaways

- Look for the lesson—especially when things don't go the way you planned.

- Until something actually happens most people think it's impossible. Believe the impossible is possible.

- No one was made to lose.

- You were born with everything you need to succeed. Use the gifts God gave you.

JIM MARKHAM'S AWARDS

Year	Award Name
2019	Intercoiffure Lifetime Achievement Icon Award
2014	BE! Beauty Entertainment Magazine
2012	Beauty Industry West Entrepreneur of the Year
2007	Ernst & Young Hall of Fame Inductee
2007	Allure Magazine—Editor's Choice Best Shampoo & Conditioner for color treated hair—PureOlogy
2007	Ernst & Young Entrepreneur of the Year for Consumer Retail Products
2007	ICMAD (Independent Cosmetic Manufacturers & Distributors) Cosmetic Innovator of the Year
2007	NAHA (North American Hairstyling Awards) Hall of Leaders
2007	Orange County Business Journal Entrepreneur of the Year
2006	Health Magazine Award—Editor's Choice Best Products
2002	ICMAD (Independent Cosmetic Manufacturers & Distributors) Entrepreneur of the Year
2002	HBA Global Award—Best Packaging Consumer Products—PureOlogy
1967	Silver Medal Winner in the Hair Styling Olympics
1967	First Place Men's Hair Styling National Championship
1967	First Place Men's Hair Styling Southwest Regional Championship
1967	First Place Men's Hair Styling Colorado State Championship
1967	First Place Men's Hair Styling New Mexico State Championship

ACKNOWLEDGMENTS

My ingredient list would be incomplete without expressing my deep gratitude to the many wonderful and talented people, who have somehow played a role in making me a winner. At the top of that list is the love of my life Cheryl Markham, who is my partner in love, life and business. You are the wind beneath my wings and have occupied that spot since our first date in 1977. You showed me with your steadfast loyalty through all my ups and downs what unconditional love and faith look like and made me trust that a partnership could work.

My children Vickie, Bobby, and Jay gave me the determination and motivation to dare to dream big and strive to set an example of success though I didn't have many around me growing up. I am thankful that we found our way back to each other. I love being your dad as well as grandad to your children Tyson, Chandler, and Leslie.

I am grateful to those long-time friends, who have become our family of the heart: Sandra Stockton and her late husband Frank and Sandra Gonzalez and Larry Knippel. You believed in Cheryl and me when we were having trouble believing in ourselves.

Jay Sebring passed on his secrets to me and trusted that I was the right one to entrust them with. He treated me as an equal and introduced me to the world of stars. He always shines in my memory.

I am eternally grateful to Paul Newman, who taught me so much — from how to treat your wife to how to savor the finer things in life. He modeled that strength and manliness could mix beautifully with kindness and compassion. Joanne Woodward has always been the epitome of graciousness and hospitality whenever Cheryl and I got to spend time in the Newmans' home. Paul's example of philanthropy inspired not only his own beautiful family, but us as well to actively seek ways to give back. Paul and I shared a love of quality products. He poured that passion into Newman's Own, which funded his passion project SeriousFun Children's Network, among others. I miss Paul, especially his pranks and sense of humor. I am grateful for our ongoing relationship with his and Joanne Woodward's daughter Clea Newman Sonderlund, who works full-time as the Ambassador for SeriousFun.

My father-in-law Dan Genis and mother-in-law Arline invested in us when we'd been turned down all over the place. I am forever grateful that you offered forgiveness and made a bet on my comeback.

Vidal Sassoon and I became friends after he'd sold his company and devoted his life to philanthropy. I had deep respect for him as a creative. That respect grew enormously as I got to know the man and his huge heart and empathy for the suffering of others.

John Paul "JP" DeJoria stands out for his generosity of spirit and willingness to help a competitor.

Danny Kopels became like a brother to me in the early days of Markham. He was willing to go on the wild ride that my dreams would take us on and bring my vision to life with his design skills. Patricia Fripp, who opened her own Markham Style Innovator Shop and traveled as a platform artist with me, helped me spread a whole new school of thought when it came to men's hair styling. Bobby Lewis had faith in us when we were at our lowest point and helped us get a fresh start. Amos Russell became a loyal friend during Sebring days and has remained a constant in our lives ever since. Thank you to Bob Clark and Rick Hough for being such great partners.

I've loved our ongoing friendship with Chuck Esserman and Yasser Toor, and have learned a great deal from both men. Thank you to all the barbers, stylists and salon owners, who listened to our stories, took the time to become educated on our products and became converts.

Our distributors have helped us build our brands and put our products into the hands of the professionals, who could show consumers what makes our products so special. I especially want to thank John and Denise Philipp, who have been great friends to us and who encouraged us to start yet another company in this business we all love.

I appreciate the chemists, the ingredient makers and producers of the essences, who have aided my education and brought me your best so that, in turn, I could conjure up the best formulas possible. Thank you to all the vendors, who help us make magic and continually up the game in hair care products. Many consultants made important contributions to our success with their advice.

To all our staff and the employees, who have been with us through our various companies, thank you for embracing our mission and supporting it.

Special thanks to Melanie A. Bonvicino for keeping it real and applying your own special brand of genius to bring this entire project together. We'd also like to thank Julie Cantrell, a gifted, thoughtful writer and editor, who provided invaluable insights, asked the right questions and helped get to the heart of the matter. Our gratitude goes to Wade Baker, who used his excellent skills as a technical editor to round up any grammatical errors or other mistakes as we worked to find the best format to sum up my life.

Writing a book takes tremendous effort and focus. It's a demanding and intimate process that requires trust and mutual respect. Cheryl and I spent a great deal of time sharing our many stories with Echo Montgomery Garrett. She also interviewed many of our colleagues, friends and family in this effort to capture the essence of my life as a serial entrepreneur. She was the chemist in this equation, who pulled all the ingredients together to create *Big Lucky*.

Reflecting on the course of my life and all the hundreds of

individuals, who believed in my dreams along the way, I am humbled and grateful.

ABOUT THE AUTHOR

Jim Markham

Multi-award-winning serial entrepreneur Jim Markham has led five successful product companies: Sebring Products, Markham Products, ABBA Pure and Natural, PureOlogy Serious Colour Care, and ColorProof Color Care Authority. He is the founder of all with the exception of Sebring Products. The combined retail sales of those companies topped $1.2 BILLION under his leadership. The award that meant the most out of the many he's  won in the course of his career was Ernst & Young Entrepreneur of the Year for Consumer Retail Products. A stylist to the stars, Jim is a self-taught chemist and has made creating breakthroughs in professional products for the hair care industry his trademark. With Markham Products, he taught a generation of men to wash and condition their hair daily and wear it natural with a cut that frames the face and emphasizes the good features. With ABBA Jim formulated the first professional product lines for women that were natural, vegan and cruelty-free. With PureOlogy Jim created the first luxury line exclusively for color-treated hair and was the first to market with sulfate-free and salt-free products.

Jim's innovation of sulfate-free has now become an industry standard worldwide in hair care and beauty products. With ColorProof, the hair care industry icon is once again upping the game with next generation super-clean, high performing products featuring breakthrough ingredient technology that include silicone-free, sulfate-free—with all of the good and none of the bad. He resides with his wife Cheryl and their dog Jagger in Orange County, California.

Follow *Big Lucky* Online

 @bigluckybook

 @bigluckybook

 @bigluckybook

Use #BigLuckyBook

Follow Jim Markham Online

 @JimMarkhamAuthor

www.JimMarkham.com

CELEBRITY CLIENT LIST

Andy Williams

Dennis Weaver

Dr. John

Eddie Fisher

Fabian

Frank Sinatra

Freddie Prinze

George Roy Hill

Henry Fonda

James Garner

Joanne Woodward

John Huston

Johnny Carson

Lee Marvin

Lee Remick

Michael Sarrazin

Paul Anka

Paul Newman

Peter Lawford

Peter Lupu

Richard Benjamin

Richard Jaeckel

Ricky Nelson

Robert Redford

Sammy Cahn

Sammy Kahn

Steve McQueen

William Holden

Wolfman Jack

INDEX

T

U

V

W

Y

ADDITIONAL REFERENCES

1: *Have Mercy!: Confessions of the Original Rock 'N' Roll Animal* by Wolfman Jack and Byron Laursen

2: *A Beautiful Business: The Maly's Story* by John Maly

Photo credits and illustrations:

All family photographs, autographed publicity stills, and the one of Jim and Jay Sebring in front of Sebring International, Albuquerque, New Mexico, courtesy Jim Markham archives.

Sebring International publicity photos.

Jim cutting Paul Newman's hair in his kitchen photographed by Kerby Smith.

Publicity photos of Jim and Peter Lawford courtesy of Markham Products.

Articles announcing Jim as the new president of Sebring, *Los Angeles Herald Examiner* and *Women's World*.

PureOlogy ad, production by Joni Rae and Associates Agency.

Jim's Unique Product Development Methodology courtesy of ColorProof.

Made in United States
North Haven, CT
21 December 2021

13501035R00163